Amana ISLAM IN AMERICA series

Muslims in America

Race, Politics and Community Building

MBAYE LO

amana publications

To
Bashir & Faizah
From
Daddy

"A ground-breaking historical account of Islam in Cleveland. I find it not only informative, but also scintillating."
— Sheikh Masoud Laryea, MA,
Hafiz Imam at large, and former Director,
Cleveland Community Islamic School

"I know of no other work that deals with the Islamic community in Cleveland with the depth and thoroughness of Mr. Lo's study. It fills a gap in the historical literature on Cleveland."
— Tom Hartshorne Ph.D.,
Professor of History,
Cleveland State University

"A long overdue document on the rich heritage of Islam in Cleveland. Mbaye did an excellent job in presenting history through an unbiased approach."
— Imam Ramez Islamboli,
President of Uqba Mosque Foundation, Cleveland

"Very informative research, accurate, and to the point. Anyone who read this work would certainly enjoy its content."
— Imam Abbas Ahmad,
Imam of the First Cleveland Mosque
President of Cleveland Council of Imams

"Eight years ago, I wrote a forward to Mbaye's Arabic book Language and Religious Themes in the African Literature in which he introduced readers of the Arab world to the cultural wealth of the African continent. Here is Mbaye again introducing readers everywhere to the history of Islam in America. This is a dynamic research and well grounded in the literature; it is a timely response to the academic community's dire need for such a multi disciplinary scholarship."
— Abdurahman A. Ousman, Ph.D.,
Chair, and Professor of Afro-Arab Studies,
Center of Research and African Studies,
International University of Africa, Khartoum, Sudan

First Edition
(1425AH/2004AC)

© Copyright 1425AH/2004AC
amana publications
10710 Tucker Street
Beltsville, Maryland 20705-2223 USA
Tel: (301) 595-5777 / Fax: (301) 595-5888
E-mail: amana@igprinting.com
Website: www.amana-publications.com

Library of Congress Cataloging-in-Publications Data

Lo, Mbaye.
  Muslims in America : race, politics, and community building / Mbaye Lo.--
1st ed.
    p. cm. -- (Amana Islam in America ; 1)
  Includes bibliographical references and index.
  ISBN 1-59008-023-8
  1. Muslims--United States. 2. Muslims--Ohio--Cleveland--History--20th century. 3. Islam--Ohio--Cleveland--History--20th century. 4. Cleveland (Ohio)--Ethnic relations--History--20th century. I. Title. II. Series.

E184.M88L6 2004
305.6'97'0973--dc22

2004001478

Printed in the United States of America by International Graphics
10710 Tucker Street Beltsville, MD 20705-2223
Tel: (301) 595-5999   Fax: (301) 595-5888
Website: igprinting.com
E-mail: ig@igprinting.com

Contents

Illustrations, Figures, and Tables vi

Acknowledgments vii

Preface 1

Chapter 1: Islam and the Muslim Community of Greater Cleveland 5
    Islam – A Conceptual Definition   5
    The Muslim Community of Cleveland   17

Chapter 2: Why Most American Converts/Reverts to Islam are
       African-Americans.. 29
    First Explanation   29
    Second Explanation   37
    The Truth Between   40

Chapter 3: Genesis of Islam in Cleveland 55
    The Ahmadiyyah Movement   56
    The First Cleveland Mosque and the MTYP   61

Chapter 4: The Muslim Experience of Black Americans 73
    Black Muslim Activism Among Black Americans   73
    Black Nationalism and Islam in Cleveland   76
    From the N.O.I. to *Sunni* Muslims   83

Chapter 5: Muslim Immigrants 89
    Reconciling Faith and Space   89
    Muslim Immigrants from Sub-Saharan Africa   91
    Muslim Immigrants from the Indian Subcontinent   94
    Muslim Immigrants from the Arab World   96

Chapter 6: Surveying the Muslim Community of Cleveland 113
    Gathering the Data   113
    Ethnic Identity, Gender and Educational Background   118
    Religious Background   122
    Religious Affiliation   124

Conclusion: Challenges and Prospective 131

Selected Bibliography 141

Index 148

Illustrations, Figures and Tables

Illustrations

Dimensions of Islamic Teachings (Page 6)

The Seven Main Beliefs of Islam (Page 7)

The Five Pillars of Islam (Page 8)

The Three Duties of a Muslim (Page 9)

The Four Sources of Islamic Teachings (Page 10)

The Three Sects of the Muslim Faith
and examples of their subdivisions (Page 14)

Figures

Ethnic Categories (Page 118)

Source of the Muslim Population (Page 120)

Others are those who do not claim American identity (Page 121)

Survey respondents who consider themselves
members in a mosque (Page 124)

Attendance among the eleven Cleveland-area mosques (Page 125)

Tables

Ethnic Categories (Page 118)

Age Category (Page 119)

Source of the Muslim Population (Page 120)

Formal Declaration of Islam (Page 122)

Cleveland area mosques' attendees distributed
across ethnic groups (Page 125)

Frequency of mosque among respondents (Page 126)

Acknowledgments

The idea behind this book goes back to 1999, when I was a graduate assistant in the History Department of Cleveland State University. I was working on my third masters degree, studying American history. Professor James Borchert, an urban historian, suggested to me that I address the need for a comprehensive study of Islam in Cleveland. "There is a lot of talk about it, but I haven't seen a single written document to support the claim," he told me in a class seminar. "Given your background and research experience, you are suitable for this research."

From then on, this project became the companion of my daily *jihad*, (struggle). I spent most of my time visiting mosques, searching archives, and interviewing community leaders and activists. In this long journey, I discovered that the history of Islam in Cleveland is a microcosm of Islam in America. On the one hand, it is the tale of American inner cities in their quest for alternative ways of life. On the other hand, it is the story of Muslim immigrants in their search for reconciliation between their homeland culture and their host land's secular space.

In dealing with this twofold story, I try to be referential when addressing historical or social events while drawing my reference from classical Islamic works to address religious issues. My ultimate goal is to invite historians and social scientists alike to study the development of Islam in the United States. Islam is increasingly becoming an inseparable part of the mainstream fabric. Any mistakes in or misinterpretations of this book are my sole misfortune, and I apologize in advance for them. As we say in Wolof, "Err is human, and perfection is divine, but humans always claim the divine's share in their infinite march toward perfection."

Although, I can't thank by name all the people who helped in my journey, I am grateful to those whose generous time and effort made this work possible. Their assistance and encouragement kept my spirit in this study alive. I wish to acknowledge Mahmud Akram, Imam Sheikh Salih Nawash, Professor Thomas Hartshorne, Tariq Salim Siyad, Khalid A. Samad, Janet Ruh, Imam Ali Omar, Professor Helen Liggett, Julie Jackson, Imam Ramiz Islamboli, Imam Abbas Ahmad, Imam Yusuf Ali, Walter Hakim Kirzy, Ahmad Said Ansari, sister Fatima Amrah, Imam Mutawaf Abdus-Shaheed, Abdurrahim Abdullah, Ahmad Fellague, Ahamd Bana, Professor Michael Tevesz and Francis Stewart.

I also would like to mention by name four individuals to whom I owe profound thanks. Without their ongoing insight, this research would have taken much more time. My deepest gratitude goes to Al-Mansur Abdur-Rahim; Sheikh Masoud Laryea, former director of the Cleveland Community Islamic School; Hayne Dyches, Ph.D., of the Cuyahoga County Community Mental Health Board; and my wife Maghboeba Mosavel, Ph.D., of Case Western Reserve University.

Preface

"I think you should all keep your good American names. I'm going to refuse the petition," stated Cleveland Probate Judge Brewer in the hot summer of 1935.

The leader of the petitioning group, James Gist, known as Jumal Ahmad, pointed out to Judge Brewer that the group from the First Cleveland Mosque was "asking the legal authority only because (they) had been advised to take this step by the board of elections since (they) had difficulties participating in any elections in the city under the [their] *Mohammedan* [Muslim] names."

"We have already spent a dollar for the legal publication," someone objected in the courtroom.

"Well, I will pay the dollar," Judge Brewer volunteered. But when someone in the group pointed out that it was one dollar for each of the eighteen petitioners, the judge changed his mind. The eighteen colored people sadly left the courtroom without legal blessing for their new Muslim names.

"These names were approved in India, 2,700 miles away," remarked one of the petitioners outside the courtroom. He was referring to the Ahmadiyyah missionaries from India, who had recruited this group to convert to Islam.

"That is 27,000 miles," corrected his wife, who joined the group to show her support.

"But to Judge Brewer, 27 feet away, they [the names] did not look so good," commented a reporter for the *Cleveland News*.[1]

In 1994, *The Plain Dealer* reported that "today there are 15 orthodox mosques in Cleveland serving 25,000 faithful, many of whom are blacks."[2]

In February 2002, the annual national convention of the Islamic Circle of North America took place in downtown Cleveland, and local reports estimated the Muslim community in the Greater Cleveland area to be about 50,000 members.

What happened during these six decades? How did this community grow from eighteen people to tens of thousands of followers? What led to the establishment of eleven mosques instead of one mosque half a century before? Answering those questions is the subject of this book.

In brief, this book uses several qualitative research methods to examine the growth of Islam in the United States in general and the history of the Muslim community in Cleveland, Ohio, in particular. The last chapter of the book is based on a survey to answer questions that would otherwise remain unanswerable. Students and colleagues often ask:

What motivates people to convert to Islam? Who introduced them to Islam?

What is the distribution of Muslims across ethnic groups and mosques?

How religious and integrated are Cleveland Muslims? Anecdotal experience is not adequate to deal with such a range of issues. Survey research offers a more reliable and objective method for answering these questions.

This is a comprehensive historical assessment of Muslim communities in Cleveland: their history, their faith and the challenges they face as they establish mosques, develop Islamic centers, and create a multi ethnic community. Currently, there are eleven community mosques in Cleveland including people of diverse cultural and ethnic backgrounds.

A historical analysis reveals three factors that have shaped, and are still shaping unevenly, the rise of Islam in Cleveland. These three factors are: (1) the Ahmadiyyah movement and its offshoot, the First Cleveland Mosque, (2) the black Muslim movement and what came of its dismantling in 1975, and (3) the Muslim immigrants. The role these factors played is not equal. The First Cleveland Mosque played a transitional role from the Ahmadiyyah movement to mainstream (*Sunni*) Islam, but the transformation of Black Muslim groups from black nationalism to *Sunni* Islam represented the main source of indigenous Muslims in this country. Muslim immigrants, however, remain the source of Islamic idealism which directs indigenous Muslims in their drive toward mainstream *Sunni* Islam.

It is my firm belief that the history of Islam in Cleveland is a local phenomenon with both national and global derivation. First, it evolved from the presence of the Ahmadiyyah movement, which arrived from India in 1920's and established the first Muslim house of worship in Cleveland. That early center was replaced by the First Cleveland Mosque under the leadership of Imam Wali Akram in 1937. Then came the ubiquitous black Muslim groups in the form of the Nation of Islam, which ended up adopting mainstream Islamic beliefs under the leadership of Imam Warith Deen Muhammad and the influence of Muslim Immigrant groups. These three groups have historically influenced the growth of Islam in Cleveland by affecting and being affected by what author Ishmael Reed called "American cultural wars."[3] From 1930 to the present, these groups have produced different segments and brands of Islam, but in the last two decades, the face of Islam and the Muslim community in Cleveland have unified toward the national trend of mainstream Islam.[4]

Notes

1. *Cleveland News* 1935 (date of the paper is missing), The First Cleveland Mosque MTYP Files.

2. *The Plain Dealer*, (August 21, 1994), p 12.

3. See Ishmael Reed, *MultiAmerica: Essay on Cultural Wars and Cultural Peace* (New York: Penguin Books, 1997).

4. Amina Nathari, *Islam In America: 1995: 20 years A.E. (After Elijah)* (New Jersey: Sabree Publication, 1995).

Chapter 1

Islam and the Muslim Communities of Greater Cleveland

> There have been Soviet Five Year Plans, and Nazi Four Year Plans. Now there comes to light a Moslem Ten Year Plan with headquarters at the Cleveland Mosque ... Head of the community, composed of Negroes, is Wali Akram, an affable, loquacious and lively man of 32.
>
> [*The Cleveland Plain Dealer*, June 20, 1937]

Islam: A Conceptual Definition

Islam is from the Arabic root word Salaam, which means peace. Etymologically, the structure of the word means the process of giving something over to someone. Thus, as religion, Islam means to give one's whole self to Allah[1], or surrender oneself for the sake of peace. A Muslim (masculine noun) or Muslima (feminine form) is one who embraces Islam, one who acts in loving obedience to Allah and believes that the Prophet Muhammad is His last and final messenger.[2]

Islamic Teachings

Islamic teachings are similar to those of Judaism and Christianity in many respects. These three religions have a common root in the Middle East. They all strive for the salvation of mankind. They are all monotheistic religions that share a belief in afterlife and, therefore, adopt rules, ethical and moral behaviors to regulate the conduct of their adherents. Like Christianity and Judaism, Islam recognizes Abraham as the father of monotheist belief and a messenger of God. However, Islam sees Jesus Christ as a prophet, not as a begotten son of God. Further, Islam consists of a set of ritual practices and ethical conducts that direct every aspect of a believer's life. This ethical conduct extends from what to say to welcome a baby in the cradle to what to say when leaving someone in his or her grave. Islam also mandates a lifetime commitment to what to do and say from dawn to dusk, such as how to sleep, how to have fun and when to have it, etc. Islamic teachings are known as *Shari'ah*, literally an eternal supply of water, and represent rules and regulations that Allah prescribes for Muslim lifestyles. The *Shari'ah* offers a detailed description of the dos and don'ts of Islam, known as *Halal* and *Haram*. The concept of complete separation between church and state or public and private does not hold in Islam.

The basic constituents of Islamic faith include seven main beliefs, five main pillars, and three main duties. These three components together constitute the abode of Islam that surrounds the life of a follower.

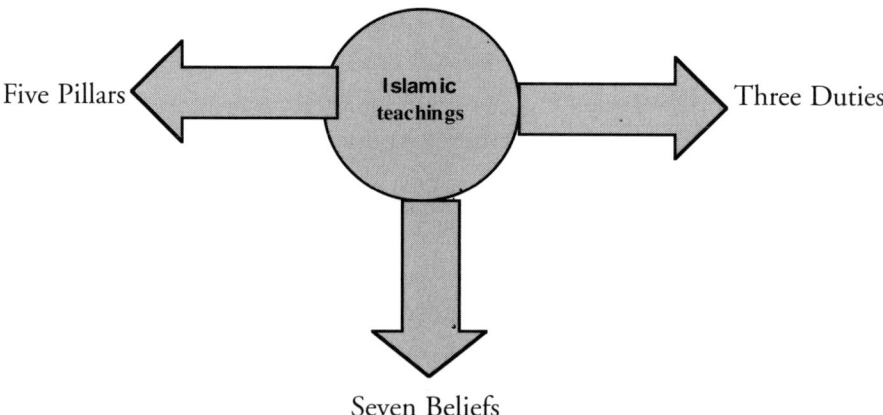

Illustration 1.1: Dimensions of Islamic Teachings

The seven main beliefs are: (1) belief in Allah, (2) belief in Allah's Angels, (3) belief in Allah's revealed books, (4) belief in Allah's messengers, (5) belief in the Judgment Day, (6) belief in Allah's decree be it good or bad, and (7) belief in life after death.[3]

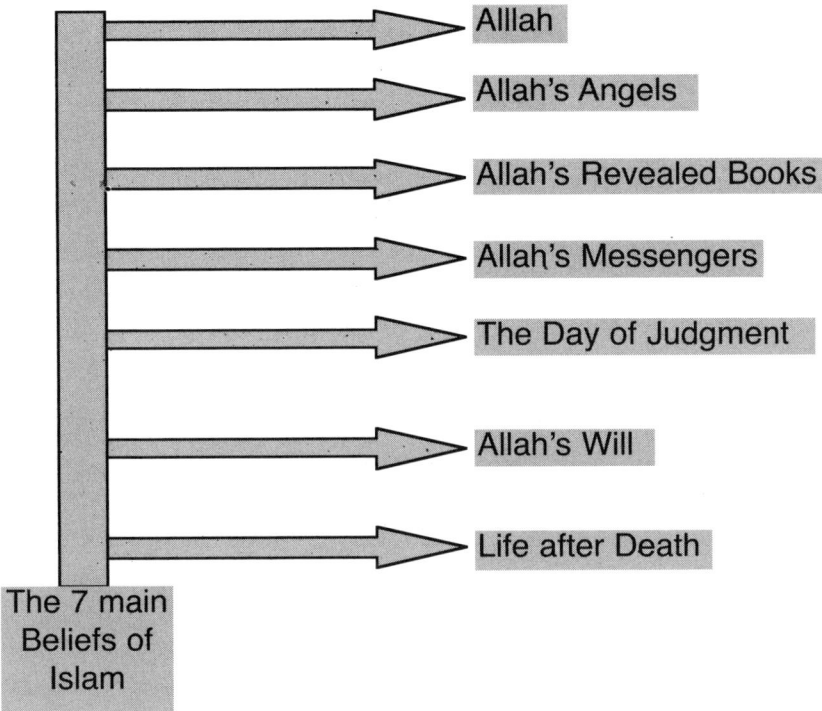

Illustration 1.2: The Seven Main Beliefs of Islam

The five doctrines, or pillars are the foundation of Islamic practices and rituals. They are:
1. Bear witness in public that there is no god but Allah, and Muhammad (pbuh) is His messenger.

This first pillar requires a constant and continuous commitment that a follower must have at every moment of his or her life. A convert to Islam must declare in front of witnesses that there is no god but Allah and Muhammad (pbuh) is Allah's last messenger.

2. Pray five times a day.

This second pillar is a lifetime commitment that a sane and age-appropriate Muslim must observe. These prayers also constitute one of the boundaries between being Muslim and non-Muslim.

3. Pay *Zakat* (tithes).

This third pillar is a yearly practice that requires from Muslims with a certain amount of wealth to give a portion (2.5 percent) of that wealth to help the needy.

4. Fasting during the month of *Ramadan*.

This fourth pillar instructs Muslims who are sane, healthy enough and over the age of puberty to fast during the month of *Ramadan*, which is the ninth month of the Islamic lunar calendar. It requires an abstinence from eating, drinking any liquid, smoking or inhaling any substance, and engaging in sexual activities from dawn to sunset every day throughout *Ramadan*.

5. Make a Pilgrimage to the Ka'ba in Mecca.

This fifth pillar is a once-in-a-lifetime commitment from Muslims to make pilgrimage to Mecca, which is in Saudi Arabia. Every sane, adult Muslim who is financially, and physically able must perform a specified journey to the Ka'ba once in his or her lifetime during the twelfth month of the Islamic lunar calendar.

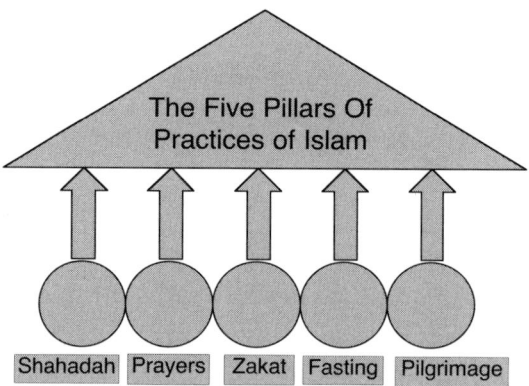

Illustration 1.3: The Five Pillars of Islam

These five pillars dictate three main duties of a Muslim. These three duties are:

1. *Da'wa*: This is the act of bringing others to Islam. The literal meaning of *Da'wa* is "to call." Therefore, calling others, regardless of their race, geographical locations, or religious affiliations, is a duty of every Muslim. *Da'wa* is achieved through personal effort of a Muslim or collective effort of a community of Muslims. However, on both levels, according to a clear verse of the Qur'an, it must not be achieved through compulsory means.[4]

2. Encouraging Good and Combating Evil: The do's and don'ts of Islam (*Halal* and *Haram*) represent the hallmarks of Muslim life. They are moral commitments to do good things, such as making the world a better place for everyone or giving to charity. There's also moral commitments to avoiding the don'ts of Islam, such as not drinking alcohol, not stealing, and not oppressing others.

3. *Jihad*: This is one of the most misinterpreted words of our time. The term means struggle in the cause of Allah. According to Islamic teachings, there are two levels of *Jihad*. The highest level is spiritual *Jihad* or self-purification. The second level is the physical *Jihad* that may involve physical struggle to combat evil. Thus, going to war to protect oneself, preserve one's property, or stop oppression against Muslims or Islam is another form of *Jihad*.

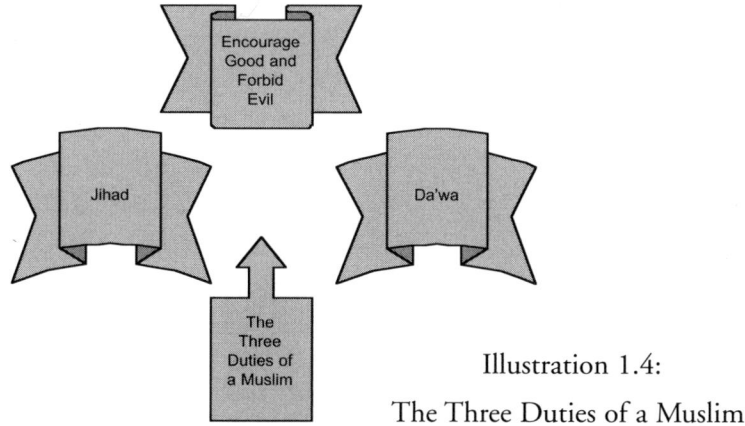

Illustration 1.4:
The Three Duties of a Muslim

These duties are ethical and moral conducts that bring together the two folds of theory and practice of the Islamic teachings. Muslims' responsibilities extend beyond themselves to the society as a whole. They must not only observe what is right and avoid what is wrong, but they must also encourage others to share that viewpoint.

Sources of Islamic Teachings

There are four hierarchically classified sources of Islamic teachings: the Qur'an, *Sunnah*, *Ijma* and *Qiyas*.

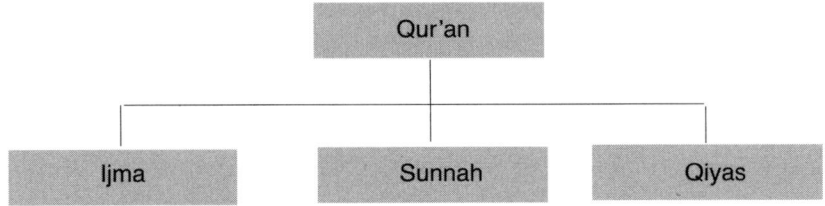

Illustration 1.5: The Four Sources of Islamic Teachings

1. The Holy Qur'an is the word of Allah put into Arabic words and revealed to the Prophet Muhammad between A.D. 610 and 630. It represents the highest authority in Islam. The Qur'an has 114 chapters, known as Surahs, comprising 6,236 verses, which make 77,437 words and 323, 671 letters.[5] It covers diverse themes, ranging from life in this world to life in the next world. It contains ancient stories, warnings, moral principles and laws. Some of these laws are clear in meaning and interpretation (*Ahkam*) such as to fast during the month of Ramadan, not to fornicate, and to help the needy. Others are allegorical (*Mutashabihat*) and need interpretations.[6]

2. *Sunnah* is the tradition of Prophet Muhammad and his companions. His words, deeds and approvals are the second source of Islamic teachings. It is also the primary source for explaining the meaning of the Qur'an. For instance, the Qur'an tells Muslims to pray but does not specify how and when. The *Sunnah* gives details on how and when to perform daily prayers.

3. *Ijma,* which is consensus, has two levels. One consists of propositions of the early companions (*Sahabah*) of the Prophet on issues not mentioned in the Qur'an or in the *Sunnah* that are binding as a source of guidance and teaching. The other consists of agreements by Muslim scholars or the *Ummah* (Muslim community), on rulings that are not explained in the two previous sources, pertaining to new situations. Examples of this include modern boundaries between countries, national identity and regulations concerning passports.

4. *Qiyas* means analogical reasoning. When the three previous sources give no clear, unequivocal judgment on new situations, Muslim scholars, *Ulama,* follow the guidelines of *Ijtihad* (independent reasoning) to relate a preceding case or principle of Islam to a new situation. For instance, marijuana is prohibited as is alcohol. The reason for prohibiting alcohol in Islam is that it has intoxicating effects on the body and mind, and proper reasoning and behavior. Because marijuana has the same effects, as alcohol the prohibition placed on alcohol also applies to marijuana.

Muslims

Islam has two definitions for Muslims. In the narrower sense, Muslim means a believer in Islam who accepts the *Shahada*, the profession of faith. In a broader sense, Islam defines Muslims as those with monotheistic beliefs. Therefore, people who share a belief in the Old Testament (i.e., Jews and Christians) are also Muslims. The Holy Qur'an classifies Christians, Jews, and Muslims in the same category, as people of divine Revelation.[7] They share a fundamental belief in monotheism as recounted in the Holy Qur'an and the Torah. Thus, Islam considers food properly prepared by Jews or Christians to be *Halal* food, or kosher food. In addition, intermarriage between male Muslims and female members of these two religions is permissible, but Muslimas (women) are required to marry within the Islamic faith.

According to Islamic teachings, every human being is a Muslim by birth because Islam is the original religion ordained for humanity from the time of creation. Therefore, Islam is the natural order. Adopting Christianity, Judaism, or other religions is a matter of socialization.[8]

Although Islamic idealism encourages all Muslims to live as one *Ummah* (faith community) and to stay away from schism and divisions, political events and ethnocentric interpretations of the Qur'an have created three major groups among the Muslims. These three groups are the *Sunni*, known as orthodox or mainstream Muslims; the *Shi'tes*; and the *Sufi*.

Sunni and *Shi'i*

Sunni literally means those who follow the path of Prophet Muhammad. *Shi'a, Shi'tes,* or *Shi'i* literally means schism and partisan. It denotes those who were partisans of Ali, the Prophet's cousin and the fourth caliph after Prophet Muhammad. There are different sects within each group; altogether, they constitute what is known as the Muslim *Ummah* (Islamic nation).

Sunnis and *Shi'is* are the two largest sects in the Muslim world. *Sunnis* make up more than two-thirds of the world's 1.3 billion Muslims. The main difference between these two groups emerged during the struggle for political power that followed the assassination of the third caliph Uthman ibn 'Affan in 656 CE (Common Era, AD). Ali ibn Abi Talib, the Prophet's cousin, succeeded Uthman, but one of Uthman's generals, Mu'awiya Ibn Abi Suffyan, who was governor of Syria, refused to recognize Ali's succession. Mu'awiya claimed that the murderers of Uthman had to be brought to justice first. In 661, Ali, who was staying in Kufa, Iraq, was murdered by a fanatic who denounced his negotiation with Mu'awiya. After the assassination of Ali, Mu'awiya easily marginalized Ali's two sons, Hassan and Hussayn, who tried in vain to succeed their father. Mu'awiya established the first Muslim empire, the Umayyah dynasty which lasted until 750. Although most Muslims accept the rule of the first four caliphs, who are known as *al khulafa ar-Rashiduna*, the *Shi'tes* denounce the chain of events that deprived Ali and his descendants of what they consider to be their right to the Muslim caliphate.[9]

A theological difference also emerged between *Sunnis* and *Shi'tes*. *Sunni* Muslims acknowledged the legitimacy of the four caliphs who came after the death of the Prophet – Abu-Bakr, Omar, Uthman, and Ali. These caliphs were chosen by consensus through a council of the elderly. Shi'te Muslims considered the first three caliphs, as well as the succeeding Ummayah dynasty, illegitimate heirs to the Muslim caliphate. *Sunnis* consider the legal judgments and jurisprudence of these four caliphs an inseparable part of *Sunna* (the second source of Islamic teachings). *Shi'tes* accept only the legal opinions of the fourth caliph Ali, and do not see other caliphs' opinions as binding source of Islamic jurisprudence.

In *Shi'a* theology, political succession is the divine right of the family of Ali [10] (the ordained family), because in *Shi'tes*'s writings, the Prophet explicitly designated Ali as his successor. *Sunni* historians denied that claim. Hussayn's martyrdom at Karbala at the hands of Yazid, son of Mu'awiya, in 680 symbolizes the rallying point among the *Shi'tes* throughout history. After the death of Hussayn, whom both *Shi'a* and *Sunni* consider "lord of the martyrs," *Shi'tes* adopted the doctrine of *Imamate*. This doctrine refers to "divinely appointed and divinely guided leaders in social, cultural, religious, and political matters in a direct line of succession from [Prophet] Muhammad."[11] The Islamic revolution in Iran in 1979 and the rise of Imam Khumayni is an example of this doctrine in practice. *Sunni* Muslims oppose the doctrine of a divine imam, and limit the Imam's role to daily prayer and counseling matters.

Sufi

Sufism is Islamic mysticism that focuses on spiritual values and the anti-establishment form of Islam. The term comes from the Arabic word *Suf* (wool), referring to the patched garment that *Sufi* mystics used to wear as a sign of asceticism. *Sufis* follow the esoteric dimension of Islam as protest against *Shi'a* political activism and *Sunni* intellectualism and institutionalism of Islam.

Unlike *Sunni*, *Sufism* internalizes the religious rituals and concepts. In some cases, Islamic concepts such as daily prayers or the notion of loving of Allah are interpreted through dance, meditation, and long periods of reflection on layers of meanings of these words. *Sufism* cuts across the two groups of *Shi'a* and *Sunni*.

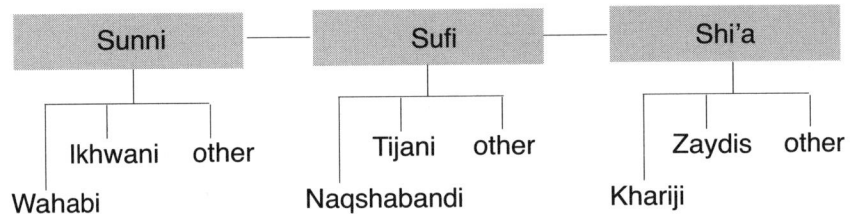

Illustration 1.6:
The Three Sects of the Muslim Faith and examples of their subdivisions

In today's world, *Sunni* Muslims are found throughout the Middle East, North, West and East Africa; and in most of Pakistan, Indonesia, Malaysia, along the southern border with Russia, and the Muslim Diaspora. *Shi'tes* are concentrated in Iran and Iraq, with pockets in North Africa, Yemen, Oman, and Pakistan.

Sufism demographically follows the same distribution as the *Shi'tes* and the *Sunni*. Additionally, it has a strong footing in Turkey, Morocco, Senegal, and among many European and Caucasian American converts.

Over the years, these three groups have produced hundreds of schools of thought that facilitated the adaptation of Islam in different places and at different times. Most importantly, these three groups created what is called *Math-hab*, or schools of thought. These schools reflect the *Fiqh*, the legal system of Islamic law established by the *Ulama*, Muslim scholars who use *Ijtihad*, independent reasoning, to compare new situations with known Islamic teachings.

There are five surviving *Math-hab* in the Muslim world. Four of them are mainly *Sunni*: *Maliki, Hanifi, Hanbali* and *Shafi'i*. One is *Shi'i*: Ja'fari.[12]

In practice, there is no major difference between the four *Sunni* schools. *Sufi* Muslims may also use any of these *Mathhib* to support their viewpoints. The leading figures in *Sufi* thought are the theosophist Muhyi al Din Ibn Al-arabi,[13] and the mystic poet Jalal al-din Ar-Rumi.[14]

The Muslim World

The term "Muslim World" refers to regions where Islam thrived historically and continues today. These regions can be classified into four areas: the Middle East, the Indian Subcontinent, the Pacific Littoral, and the Sahelian and Saharan Africa.

The Middle East and North Africa

Three factors are basic to understanding Islam in these two regions. First, the Middle East is the birthplace of the three monotheistic religions – Judaism, Christianity, and Islam. Second, all countries of the Middle East and North Africa are Arabic-speaking except Iran, Turkey, and Israel. Third, all countries of the two regions are dominated by Islam except Israel. In fact, in all the Arab countries excluding Lebanon, Muslims make up more than ninety percent of the total population.

The Indian Subcontinent

This is the region with the largest Muslim population in the world. The Muslim countries of this region are Pakistan and Bangladesh. Pakistan, which literally means holy land, was created in 1947 as a homeland for the Muslims of India, and has a total population that is more than ninety-six percent Muslim. Bangladesh separated from Pakistan in 1971 has a population more than ninety percent Muslim.

The Pacific Littoral

This is the most eastern Muslim region. It includes Indonesia, which is the most populous Muslim country, and Malaysia, which is one of the most technologically advanced among Muslim countries. In both countries, Muslims are over eighty percent of the total population.

Sahelian and Saharan Africa

This region extends from the Atlantic Ocean to the Lake Chad area. Islam reached this region at the turn of the eleventh century. In most of these African countries, Muslims make up more than eighty percent of the population.

The Muslim Diaspora

In addition to these traditional population centers, hundreds of millions of Muslims are dispersed in other parts of the world. More than fifty million Muslims are in China, two hundred million in India, ten million in the Americas, twelve million in Western Europe and three million in South Africa. Additional concentrations are found in the Balkans and in the countries along the southern border of Russia.

The Muslim Community of Cleveland

Islam is the fastest growing religion in the United States. Because the U.S. Census Bureau does not identify religious affiliation, there is no official account for the number of Muslims in this country. According to a publication of the American Muslim Council (AMC), the number of Muslims in the United States was five million in 1992, and seven million in 1996 and eight million in 1999. The Arab American institute reported that in 1970 there were only 500,000 Muslims in this country. The number of mosques rose from 598 in 1986 to 1,372 in 2001.[15] In 1993, Paul Martinson estimated the number of mosques and Islamic centers in the United States to be 1,100, and eighty percent of the mosques has been established within the last twelve years.[16] Most of these mosques and Islamic centers are associated with local or national organizations that promote Islamic views on moral, social, and political issues.

Mosque: Center of Faith and Space

The mosque, or *masjid* in Arabic, represents the core of the Muslim community. The term mosque refers to a center of worship where Muslims congregate, pray, read the Holy Qur'an, and further their knowledge of Islam. The primary mission of a mosque is to offer Muslims, regardless of gender or race, a congregational space for prayer services. According to the Qur'an, which is the highest legal opinion in Islamic jurisprudence, mosques are built only for the sake of worshiping Allah and nothing else.[17]

The mosque, however, serves as the center of all community activities. In traditional Muslim societies, mosques are generally built or sponsored by wealthy individuals or governments. The role of the mosque ranges from specialized education – called *madrasa* in southeast Asia, *khalwa* in North Africa, and *dara* in the western African region – to social and commercial purposes.

There tend to be two types of mosques in traditional Muslim societies. The street mosque, generally known as *Masjid*, is convenient for nearby residents to perform their daily prayers. This type of mosque is primarily founded and maintained by local communities and is the focus of community activities. Marriage contracts, in most cases, are first performed there before they reach the legal authorities. Family and neighborhood disputes are also settled by the imam. Events such as births, deaths, and engagements are announced after prayers. Contrary to Islamic teachings, which prohibit turning women away from mosques, most street mosques throughout the Muslim world do not include space for women. As such, street mosques have been transformed into male places of business that are unfriendly to women worshippers.

Masjid al-Jami'h, or grand mosque, is where the local communities, regardless of their street mosques, meet together during *Jumu'ha*, *Eid al-fitr*, and *Eid al-adha* prayers.[18] Such mosques are also known as state-sponsored mosques and are primarily under state authority.[19] Female worshippers are expected in the grand mosques, therefore, space is provided for women.

In North America, due to the low Muslim population density and the fact that few adherents to Islam are able to attend daily prayers in mosques, there tends to exist only one type of mosque to serve all prayer and community related purposes. Therefore, there is no distinction between street and *jami'h* mosques. In this sense, the term mosque, or *Masjid*, refers to the center of worship where Muslims congregate, perform ritual prayers and read Islamic scriptures. In the last two decades, thousands of mosques were established in the United States as a result of migration, immigration and growth in Muslim population.

Different mosques may have different rules on such issues as separating the sexes. Some specify an upper level for women or use curtains to separate male and female worshippers. Others might have a less strict separation. For instance, allowing women to pray in the rear of the same space as men. These differences stem from whichever school of Islamic jurisprudence the community mosque has adopted.

The heterogeneity of these different rules reflects the flexibility of Islam in accommodating individual and group choices within the abode of its teachings. Thus, immigrants can find in the mosque a space for self-preservation and cultural attachment to their homeland. This explains an ethnic group's connection to a particular mosque for cultural purposes or socialization. Some mosques are frequently attended by a particular ethnic group, such as Pakistanis, Palestinians, or African-Americans because of historical coincidence of how a particular ethnic group's idea of the mosque started or because of the mosque's geographical reality such as accessibility from the group's neighborhood. But under no religious interpretation should an ethnic group's connection to a particular mosque result in naming the mosque after that particular ethnic group such as Arab mosque, black mosque, or Indo-Pakistani mosque. The Holy Qur'an makes it clear that piety comes before nationality, race, class, and status. There should be equality among all people.[20]

Although the first mosques were mostly converted church and synagogue buildings in the African-American Muslim community, new mosques are built as repository of authentic Islamic architecture and Muslim identity.

Besides the obligatory design requirements of a mosque, such as a distinguishing tower (*minaret*), an orienting *mihrab* in the *Qiblah* wall (*Qiblah* is direction of Mecca, southeast from the United States), a *minbar* for oration (*khutbah*) at Friday and *Eid* prayers, a prayer place alongside it, and facilities for restrooms and ritual ablution, the new diaspora mosques set aside either a mezzanine, an upper floor, or a separate side hall for women. The new masjids or Islamic centers also have taken into account the need for lecture halls, meeting rooms, and sometimes Islamic schools. Mosques, however, should be free of decoration, pictures, or anything that interferes with worshippers' devotion to God.

Cleveland Community Mosques

In Cleveland, at present only three out of the eleven community mosques covered in this study were built from the ground up.

Masjid Bilal was the first mosque in Cleveland to be built from the ground up. The building was completed in 1982, sponsored primarily by boxing champion Muhammad Ali and Imam Warith Deen Muhammad. The mosque features a ceremony room and meeting spaces. Women use the rear area of the same praying place.

Masjid Bilal on East 75th Street and Euclid Avenue.
Imam: Clyde Rahman

The Islamic Center of Cleveland is the largest mosque in northeast Ohio and one of the hallmarks of Islamic architecture in the United States. The building was a homemade project made possible primarily through fund-raising led by a Palestinian gynecologist, Dr. Azzam Ahmad. The building was inaugurated in February 1995. It has an upper-level section for women. In 1999 a weekend Islamic school was added to the building.

The Islamic Center of Cleveland on 6055 W.130 Street.
Imam: Fawaz Damra

The Uqbah Mosque was completed in 2000. It was sponsored through community fund raisers and a $200,000 donation from the Zayed Foundation of United Arab Emirates. The mosque has an upper floor as a specified space for women. The building also includes a library, activity rooms, and a weekend Islamic school.

Uqbah Mosque Foundation on 2227 Petrarca Road. President: Imam Ramiz Al-Istamboli

Masjid Al-Haqq on 1187 Hayden Avenue. Imam: Daud A. Malik

This former Presbyterian Church was first transformed into a rehabilitation center which grew out of the Black Unity House created by Larry Thomas, a black activist in the 1970s. He became Muslim in the following years and adopted the Muslim name of Daud Abdul Malik. After he founded the Universal Muslim Brotherhood, the building became the community mosque known as Masjid Haqq or Masjid Al-Haqq. Women members use the rear area of the main praying space.

Masjid Al-Islam
on 4600 Rocky River Drive.
Founding Imam: Sheik Saleh Nawash

Masjid Al-Islam moved to this former church in 2000. The mosque has a specified space for women. In fall 2001, the Ihsan Islamic School was started in the same building to provide kindergarten and first-grade education to children.

Masjid Al-Mu'min moved to this former funeral home in 1975. Women members use the rear area of the main praying space.

Masjid Al-Mu'min
on 2690 M.L.K. Jr. Drive.
Imam: Mutawaf Abdus-Shaheed

Masjid An-Nur, a converted residence, was founded in 1974. It has a separate space for women.

Masjid An-Nur on 1253 East 99th Street. Imam: Yunus Muhammad

Masjid Ummatullah is a street mosque that tends to relocate very often in the inner city. This mosque is the smallest of eleven orthodox Muslim communities. It has a separate space for women.

Masjid Ummatullah on 3929 East 140th St.
Imam: Abdul Sulayman Malik

First Cleveland Mosque
on 3613 East 131st Street.
Imam: Abbas S. Ahmad.

The First Cleveland Mosque is housed in a building that was a Slovakian community house since 1975. It consists of several offices, classrooms, and a basement for ceremonial activities. Women use the rear area of the main praying space. In the fall of 2001, the Cleveland Community Islamic School (CCIS) relocated from Masjid Warith Deen Muhammad on Superior Avenue to the First Cleveland Mosque building. CCIS provides first, through ninth-grade education. The First Cleveland Mosque's previous three locations after its separation from the Ahmadiyyah movement in 1937 were: 7605 Woodland Avenue from 1939 to1966, 12715 Miles Avenue from 1966 to 1969, and 13405 Union Avenue from 1969 to 1975.

Masjid Warith Deen on 7301 Superior Ave.
Imam: Yusuf A. Ali

The community moved into this former Youth Community Center in 1992. The facility continues to provide community services such as free meal programs and providing weekend Islamic classes. The building includes classrooms and meeting rooms. Women worshippers use the rear area of the main prayer space.

MACE Mosque
on 25900 Chardon Road,
Richmond Heights.
President: Ahmad Bana

The Muslim Association of Cleveland East (MACE) started in 1997 in the hands of few Muslim professionals who were rotating their houses and offices as prayer places. In 2000, the group purchased this current building, which was formerly a lawyer's office, to be used as the community mosque. The Mosque also administers a weekend Islamic school

Cleveland's mosques represent the collective identity of the local Muslim community. The history of each mosque embodies the story of its founders. Within the African-American Muslim community, three models of creating a mosque can be identified.

In one model, a missionary group or a group with a distinct ideology came to Cleveland and started introducing Islam to the neighborhood. The group rented a place as headquarters and a house of worship for the congregation and changed the name of the site or house to reflect its new identity.

In the second model of mosque building, a Nation of Islam Temple or a black nationalist organization transformed teachings from black nationalist ideology to orthodox Islam and rented or built a new site to reflect its adopted ideology.

In the third model, an internal conflict in mosque administration or different ideology adopted by the leadership drove a group to disassociate itself from the mosque, rent a site for religious services, and finally, construct a mosque for the new community.

These three forms of mosque building are common in the African-American community. The First Cleveland Mosque, Masjid Ummatullah and Masjid An-Nur fit into the first model. Masjid Bilal and Masjid Al-Haqq are examples of the second model. Masjid Warith Deen and Masjid Al-Mumin fit into the third model.

There are also three models for establishing mosques in the Muslim immigrant community:

In the first models, several Muslim families came together for ritual services, rotated from house to house during *Jumu'ah* prayers, rented a site to accommodate their growing numbers, nominated an imam to lead the prayers and coordinate their worship activities, and finally constructed a mosque.

In the second model, an internal conflict occurred in the administration of the mosque, a group disassociated itself from the mosque, rented a site for religious services and finally constructed a new mosque for the newly established community.

As a part of the third method, foreign Muslim students created Islamic study groups at a university campus. As members increased, the group created a local chapter of the national Muslim Student Association (MSA), extended MSA activities to the local communities to accommodate graduating members, rented a site off campus for weekend organized activities and finally built a mosque for the newly established community.

All these models of establishing mosques exist within the Muslim immigrant community of Cleveland. The Islamic Center of Cleveland and the Muslim Association of Cleveland East (MACE) represent the first model. Masjid Al-Islam represents the second model, and Masjid Uqbah fits into the third model.

Notes

1. Translating *Allaahu*, Allah into God is a misinterpretation of religious culture. Unlike Allah, the word god can refer to a false god. There is no word in any language other than Arabic that fully overlaps with the concept of Allah. Indeed, the term Allah reveals for a believer other attributes, such as *ar-rahamaan* (Beneficent), *ar-raheem* (Merciful), *al-qayyuum* (Sustaining), etc.

In the Islamic sciences, *Allaahu* is seen as the most sacred of the ninety-nine names given in the Qur'an (66:110). A person cannot substitute any other name in the *shahaadah*, the first pillar in Islam by which one becomes a Muslim, i.e., *laa ilaaha illa Allaahu*, not *la ilaaha illa al-kareemu*, etc. It is also the only name used in the call for prayer five times a day, *Allaahu akbaru*.

In Arabic language, *Allaahu* is the only name that remains meaningful even if one or more of its letters are dropped. If we drop the first letter sound, *alif*, the name is *lillaahi*, (for or to Allaah, a meaningful term that is found in several verses of the Qur'an. If we drop the first "L" sound, *laam*, we are left with *lahu* (for Him). If we drop the final *laam*, we are left with *huu* (Him) or *huwa* (He), which has its significance in mysticism.

Moreover, though the word *Allaahu* is used in the language as a second or third term of *idaafah* (construction), it can never be used as a first term.

2. In the Islamic teachings, it is obligatory to say, "Peace Be Upon Him" (pbuh), whenever the name of the Prophet Muhammad is mentioned.

3. These seven beliefs are called "the detailed belief." See Qur'an: 4:136.

4. Qur'an 2:256: "There is no compulsion in matters of religion".

5. See Yahiya Emerick, *What Islam Is All About* (New York: International Book and Tapes Supply, 1997)

6. As an example of this: Qur'an says, "The Most Gracious is firmly established on the throne [of authority]" (20:5). This verse is one of the Mutashabihats. What is the nature of Allah's actions, such as sitting on a throne? Our intellect as human is limited in conceptualizing this meaning.

7. Qur'an 42:13.

8. In an authentic *Hadith*, the Prophet of Islam states, "Every child is born following his or her natural inclination [Muslim]. It is the parents who make him or her a Jew, a Christian, or Zoroastrian [the Old Persian religion that worships fires]." See Ibn Al-hajar Al-'sqalani, *Fathul-Bari* (Egypt, Cairo: Maktab Kulliyat Al-Azar, 1987), p. 127.

9. For more on *Shi'a* history and theology, read Allamah Sayyid Muhammad Husayn Tabatab'i, *Shite Islam*. Translated by Seyyed Hossein Nasr (New York: State University of New York Press, 1975), p. 41.

10. Ali was married to the only surviving daughter of Prophet Muhammad (pbuh). Therefore, Hassan and Hussayn were the only two grandsons of the Prophet Muhammad.

11. George Fry and James R. King, *Islam: A Survey of the Muslim Faith* (Michigan: Baker Book House, 1980), 116.

12. These names reflect the names of the founders: *Maliki* (Imam Malik Ibn Anas was born in Arabia, 711-795); *Hanifi* (Imam Abu Hanifa was born in Iraq, 700-768); *Hanbali* (Imam Ahmad ibn Hanbal was born in Arabia, 780-855); *Ash-Shafi'i* (Imam Muhammad Ash-Shafi'i was born in Palestine, 767-820), and *Ja'fari* (Imam Ja'far as Sadiq was born in Arabia, 699-765).

13. Al-arabi was born in Spain between 1165 and 1240.

14. Ar-Rumi was born in Khurasan, Iran 1207-1273.

15. For more on U.S. Muslim statistics, see Paul Findley, *Silent No More* (Maryland: Amana Publication, 2001), 39-43.

16. Paul Varo Martinson, *Islam: An Introduction for Christians* (Translated by Stefanie Ormsby Cox. Minneapolis: Augsburg, 1994), 91.

17. Qur'an, 72:18.

18. *Jumu'ha*, or Friday prayer, is a noon prayer with a sermon that is supposed to review current religious, social and political events of the week.

Eid-al-fitr is the celebration of breaking the fast which marks the end of the month of *Ramadan*.

Eid-al-adha is the festival of sacrifice that celebrates the last four days of the pilgrimage to Mecca. Muslims worldwide are encouraged to sacrifice a sheep, cow or goat and share the meat with friends and the needy.

19. Since the rise of Islamic revivalist movements in the Muslim world and mosques have become the only public space for anti-state activities, government are increasingly putting street mosques under state authority. For instance, Egypt, Morocco, Algeria, Tunisia and Oman have adopted laws that regulate and control all mosque activities.

20. Qur'an, 49:13.

Chapter 2

Why Most American Converts/Reverts are African-Americans[1]

> Blacks originally adopted Islam to satisfy their need for cultural identity. But the Black Muslim movement today also embraces revolutionary social demands for blacks.
>
> [*The Cleveland Press*, October 19, 1974]

In recent years, there has been a growing academic inquiry into the social, historical, and political motivation of African-American conversion or reversion to Islam. Although African-Americans make up only twelve percent of the total American population, they represent more than one-third of the estimated seven million U.S. Muslims.[2] In Steven Barboza's 1994 study, eighty-five to ninety percent of are African-Americans.[3] In the most comprehensive survey of U.S. Muslims, Professor Ihsan Bagby of Shaw University in Raleigh, North Carolina, found that out of 19,706 converts, 13,783 were African-American, 4,110 were white, 1,209 were Hispanic and Latinos, and 604 were of other ethnic background.[4] Within academic inquiries and American Muslim writings two basic explanations of this phenomenon emerge. I will discuss the main points in each explanation before offering my conclusion on this subject.[5]

First Explanation

One school of thought proposes that the spread of Islam in the African-American community ought to be interpreted from a broad historical perspective that embodies all people of West African descent in the New World.⁶ This is because what Europeans consider the golden age of slavery (1500 to 1800) coincided with the rise of Islam and Muslim kingdoms in West Africa. This region, extending from the Gambia River to the Gulf of Guinea, was known among the European adventurers as the Gulf of Slavery. Therefore, the hypothesis that many slaves were already Muslims before their resettlement in the New World is irrefutable. Sylviane Diouf gives this account of what happened in the southern plantations:

> The newly arrived slaves were given strange names by their owners, in a move whose intention was not only for the convenience of slaveholder but also an attempt to annihilate their past, sense of self, culture, kinship, ethnic origin, and religion.⁷

Terry Alford notes that the existence of Islam and Muslims among the African slaves was common knowledge among slaveholders:

> Each slave holder was pretty well free to do what he wished about Islamic practice on his plantation. It could be an important decision. The annual fast [month of Ramadan], the dietary rules [not eating pork], and the work lost due to frequent prayers of practicing Muslims required forbearance from an owner.⁸

A slave called Omar ibn Said recalled in his autobiography of 1831:

> Before I came to the Christian country my religion was the religion of Mohammed [Islam], the Apostle of Go – May God have mercy upon him and give him peace! I walked to the mosque before day-break, washed my face and head, hands and feet [ablution], I prayed at noon, prayed in the afternoon, prayed at sunset, prayed in the evening. I gave alms every year.... I went on pilgrimage to Mecca.... When I left my country I was thirty-seven years old; I have been in the country of the Christians twenty-four years.⁹

Why Most American Converts are African-Americans

After staying in this country for twenty-four years, Omar had converted to Christianity. He recounts his story:

> When I was a Muhammadan I prayed thus: "Thanks be to God, Lord of all Worlds, the merciful, the gracious, Lord of the day of Judgment, thee we serve, on thee we call for help,"...but now I pray, "Our Father"...in the words of our Lord Jesus the Messiah.[10]

Until the Civil War in 1861, it was common among slaveholders to address runaway slaves under two names: a Muslim name, which the slave had in Africa, and the master's name, which was given to the slave by the slaveholder. Arabic language, which is a vital component of all Muslim societies, was familiar among enslaved Africans in the Carolina region.[11]

Historically, West Africa has been attached to Islam since the rise of the empire of Ghana in the eleventh century. An eleventh century Arab historian, Al-Bakri (1067-8), described Ghana, which was exercising control over a wide expanse of territory from the edge of the Sahara, south into the Niger region and west to the Senegal River, saying, "The king's conduct is praiseworthy, being a lover of justice and favorable to Muslims."[12] The Mali Empire came in the aftermath of Ghana and its greatest ruler, Mansa Musa (1312-37), visited Mecca for pilgrimage. In his time, Islam spread from the upper Niger in the north to the Atlantic area in the west. Ibn Battuta, an Arab traveler and an eyewitness [of Mali before] Mansa Musa, described the empire as such: "The Muslim leaders had an official status at the court and were present at royal audiences. The king and all members of the court took part in the public prayers held at the two great Islamic festivals."[13]

Three major empires succeeded Mali in ruling the West African region until the rise of the transatlantic slave trade which operated from 1500 to 1830. Ironically, all three empires were described by eyewitness historians as Islamic in their law, governance, and population. Professor John Hunwick of Northwestern University calls the epoch between 1494 and 1591 the tenth Islamic century in West Africa.[14] These three empires – Songhay, Bornu and Housaland – established international relationships across the desert to promote education and literacy in major educational centers such as Timbuktu, Kano, Gao and Jen.

The following piece written by a Timbuktu scholar Abdal-Rahman-al-Sa'di in 1613 illustrates the life and literacy of the city. He described a Timbuktu scholar by the name of Muhammad Abi Bakr al-Wangari, known as Baghayogho:

> The jurist and accomplished scholar, a pious and ascetic man of God, who was among the finest of God's righteous servants and practicing scholars. He was a man given by nature to goodness and benign intent, guileless, and naturally disposed to goodness, believing in people to such an extent that all men were virtually equal in his sight, so well did he think of them and absolve them of wrongdoing. Moreover, he was constantly attending to people's needs, even at cost to himself, becoming distressed at their misfortunes, mediating their disputes, and giving counsel.[15]

Another example from al-Sa'di describes a scholar by the name of Qadi Mahmud:

> [Mahmud] devoted himself to teaching. Jurisprudence from his mouth had a sweetness and elegance, his easy turn of phrase making the subject wonderfully clear without affectation. Many people benefited from him. He revived scholarship in his land, and the number of students of jurisprudence increased, some of them showing brilliance and becoming scholars. The books he most frequently taught were the *Mudawwana*, the *Risala*, the *Mukhtasar* of *Khalil*, the *Alfiyya*, and the *Salalijiyya*[16] ...One of his students put together a commentary in two volumes, based on notes taken from his teaching.[17]

During the succeeding three centuries of transatlantic slave trade, these regional empires amalgamated into local Islamic kingdoms that coexisted with non-Islamic influenced kingdoms, such as Dahomey, the Yoruba Kingdom of Oyo, and the Kingdom of Sin in the Senegambia region.

In Hausaland, nowadays northern Nigeria and Niger, Sheikh Usman Dan Fodio (1754-1817) led a puritan movement of Islam and successfully established the Sokoto Caliphate in 1808. This caliphate ruled northern Nigeria until its demolishment at the hands of the British in 1903. In 1776, Abdel Kader Kane and Sulayman Bal established the reformist Islamic state of Futa Toro between Guinea, Mali, and Senegal. In the mid-nineteenth century, Al-Hajj Omar Tal (1794-1864) also renewed the legacy of Abdel Kader Kane in establishing an Islamic rule in the Futa Toro area. A. Adu Boahen, a leading African historian from Ghana provides this picture:

> But nowhere in the social field had more changes occurred by 1880 than in the field of religion. As result of a series of *jihads* in Hausaland under the leadership of Usman dan Fudio in 1804, in Masina under the leadership of Sheikh Ahmadu in 1818, and in the Bambara area under the leadership of Sheikh Umar, or al Hadi Umar, in 1852 all with primary aim of spreading and purifying Islam – that Middle East religion, which had been introduced into Africa in the seventh century A.D., had spread into areas hitherto untouched. Thus, by 1880, Islam in the Western Sudan [West Africa] had been converted from a religion of the urban and trading centers and court circles into that of the rural areas as well.[18]

This history is reflected in today's West African region, where Muslims are the majority of the population. For instance, the four major ethnic groups of West Africa are predominantly Muslims: Hausa, in mainly Nigeria, Niger and Ghana is ninety percent Muslim.

Mandingo, known as *Jula* in the Ivory Cost, Ghana and Burkina, are ninety percent Muslim. Mandingo resides primarily in Mali, Guinea, and the Senegambia area. Yoruba in Nigeria and Benin is fifty percent Muslim.[19] Fulani, between the Senegalese River and Lake Chad is ninety-five percent Muslims. These facts are not a modern phenomenon; in 1606, Father Barreira of Portugal was a missionary who visited these regions and pointed out:

> Fulos … [Fulani] follow the sect of Muhamet [Islam]…the Jalofo [Wolof] follow the law of Mahomet…the Berbeci…[berber] follow [the] law of Mahomet…the Mandingas [Mandingo] follow the sect of Mahomet.[20]

The Islamic dominance in the West African population was not unfamiliar to the early European administrators of this region or to the early African-American repatriates to Africa, such as Edward W. Blyden (1832-1912) and W. E .B. Du Bois (1868-1963).

In 1913, William Ponty, the lieutenant governor of the French colonies of West Africa, called his European colleagues to acknowledge and study the reality of Islam in West Africa. He noted:

> It is almost impossible to administer an Islamic people wisely, if one does not understand its religious faith, its judicial system, and its social organization which are all intimately connected and are strongly influenced by the Coran and the prophet tradition.[21]

Edward W. Blyden was one of the most acclaimed pioneers of African rights in the diaspora. He traveled and wrote extensively about the theme of return to Africa. He spent the rest of his life in Sierra Leone, studying the geopolitics and the socio-cultural life of the West African region.

In 1888, Blyden published his most comprehensive essays concerning the region in a book titled *Christianity, Islam, and the Negro Race*. In this book, he reported:

Muhammadanism (Islam) found its Negro converts at home in a state of freedom and independence of the teachers who brought it to them. When it was offered to them they were at liberty to choose for themselves. The Arab missionaries, whom we have met in the interior, go about without "purse or scrip" and disseminate their religion by quietly teaching the Koran. The Native missionaries – Mandingoes and Foulahs – unite with the propagation of their faith active trading. Whenever they go, they produce the impression that they are not preachers only, but traders; but on the other hand, that they are not traders merely, but preachers. And in this way, silently and almost unobtrusively, they are causing princes to become obedient disciples and zealous propagators of Islam.[22]

Like Blyden, W. E. B. Du Bois, who was a founding member of the National Association for the Advancement of Colored People (NAACP) and who was one of the most prolific writers of African descent in the twentieth century, did not see a paradox between Islam and people of African descent. Despite his socialist affiliation, he gave a fair assessment of Islam in West Africa. In 1961, he joined the Communist Party of the United States, and in the same year, he immigrated to Ghana, where he became a full citizen. In his 1930 booklet on Africa, its geography, people, and products, Du Bois wrote:

> Islam never conquered the black Sudan, but it converted and transformed it. Arabic became the lingua-franca and a series of Negro kingdoms arose, organized and governed by black men, who professed the Muhammadan religion [Islam], and acknowledged the suzerainty of Mecca.[23]

These perceptions of Islam and the Africans had no effect on the line of inquiry concerning the African-American converts until mid-1984. That year, Allan Austin, a professor of English and

African-American studies at Springfield College in Massachusetts, published a 759-page groundbreaking source book on African Muslims in antebellum America. A self-explanatory work that presented primary writings, documents, biographies, and autobiographies of Muslim slaves of the antebellum South.[24] This book awakened a popular and academic interest in the history of Islam in the African diaspora.

In the mid-1990's several studies started exploring the scope of Muslim presence in antebellum America. In 1995, Adib Rashaad, formerly known as James Miller, published a dynamic research titled *Islam, Black Nationalism and Slavery: A Detailed History*. The book shed light on the triangular relationship between Islam, black nationalism, and slavery. The author extensively used classical references to make a connection between Islam and Africa and then Islam and black nationalism. He concluded that Islam did not represent a strange culture in the eye of African-Americans. Islam was known to their ancestors in Africa and was a vital component of the black nationalist movements of the New World.

In a 1997 publication, Imam Abdullah Hakim Quick, known as the first American graduate of the Islamic University of Madinah, in Saudi Arabia, who earned his doctorate from the University of Toronto, Canada, offered an eccentric view of Islam in the Americas. In his view, "Islam has been in America from before the founding of the thirteen colonies, but Muslims have never played a recognizable part in the development of our society."[25]

One of the most objective and resourceful materials in this regard was published in 1998 by the West African academic Dr. Sylviane Diouf. The book, titled *Servants of Allah: African Muslims Enslaved in the Americas*, gives a cogent account of the recount between West African Muslims and the institutions of slavery in the New World. Contrary to mainstream writers in this domain, Diouf explores how educated a large number of these slaves were and how

deep their Islamic influence on certain cultural and religious aspects of the Americas is.[26] In the same year, Amir Nashid Ali Muhammad published a book titled *Muslims in America: Seven Centuries of History (1312-2000)* to claim that Islam was in the Americas prior to the arrival of Christopher Columbus in the fifteenth century.[27]

In short, this explanation posts that Islam is not a foreign religion to the Africans of North America. It is the religion of most of their ancestors in Africa. Imam Warith Deen Mohammed, leader of the largest African-American Muslim community in the U.S. explains African-American conversions to Islam: "Scores of men and women re-claimed the original way of life that their ancestors had before being brought to America."[28]

Second Explanation

This group of mostly social scientists considers the tendency toward Islam among African-Americans to be an identity issue generated by years of subjugation to slavery, racism, and striking poverty. The Nation of Islam (N.O.I.), the first popular Muslim movement of black Americans, symbolizes the apex of this search for identity. Elijah Muhammad, who led the N.O.I. for more than 40 years, was not an orthodox Muslim, but rather a *proto Islam*, to use Eric Lincoln's words.[29] What attracted thousands to Elijah Muhammad's message was not the Muslim religion itself, but rather the nationalistic rhetoric of racial superiority of blacks that permeated the N.O.I. The core of the Nation of Islam's belief was racial superiority of being black. Elijah Muhammad clarified his theology stating:

> The original man, Allah has declared, is none other than the black man. The black man is the first and last, maker and owner of the universe. From him came brown, yellow, red, and white people. By using a special method of birth control law, the black man was able to produce the white race.... The white race is not, and never will be, the chosen people of Allah. They are the chosen people of their father Yakub, the devil.[30]

Professor E.U. Essien-Udom was among the first academicians to call attention to the phenomenon of Islam in the African-American community. After spending two years within the Nation of Islam in the1950's, he published a comprehensive study on the organization, claiming "the need for identity and the desire for self improvement are the two principal motives which lead individuals to join and to remain in the Nation of Islam."[31]

Some renowned writers, such as James Baldwin, John Henrik Clarke, Chancellor Williams, Molefi Kete Asante, Bernard Lewis, and Allan Fisher, directly or indirectly shared this view. James Baldwin, a novelist and prolific writer of the Civil Rights Movement, disagreed with Malcolm X's views on Islam, which he saw as "not relevant in the African American experience."[32] Baldwin protested against black conversion to Islam. He noted that "the Negro has been formed by this nation, for the better or for the worse, and does not belong to any other – not to Africa, and certainly not to Islam."[33]

John Henrik Clarke, a vocal and an accomplished African-American historian and writer who died in 1998, advocated that there was no room for Islam in the African history because Islam was imposed on Africans by Arabs who were also foreign invaders. He notes:

> [Arab invaders] looked with disdain on all African ways of life alien to their understanding. These invaders made every effort to destroy the confidence of African people and the image of God as Africans originally conceived God to be. In large areas of Africa, Africans stopped worshipping a god of their own choosing and stopped speaking of God in a language of their own making.[34]

Chancellor Williams, a noted African-American historian in the post civil rights era, considered African-American conversion/reversion to Islam a grave confusion of the identity search. He noted:

Blacks in the United States seem to be more mixed up and confused over the search for racial identity than anywhere else. Hence many are dropping their white western slave masters' names and adopting, not African, but their Arab and Berber slave masters' names.[35]

The late Afrocentrists also challenged the phenomenon of Islam in the African-American community. Professor Molefi Kete Asante of Temple University acknowledged the reality of Islam in Africa, but questioned what made Islam as well as other religions, more important than traditional African practices: "I do not know what constitutes their greatness, that is, any more than the greatness, say of Oduduwa of the Yoruba, Okomfo of the Asante, or Chaminuka of the Shona."[36]

Professor Bernard Lewis of Princeton University is a prominent American historian and a Middle East expert. In his view, black identity search in Islam is a fallacy and cannot be sustained from a historical viewpoint for a very simple fact:

> The culture role of blacks in medieval Arab Islam was small, as compared with the role of the Arabs, Persians, and Turks, of minor significance. It was primarily as slaves that they were imported to the Islamic lands, and it was as slaves of various kinds that they rendered their service to Islam.[37]

Allan Fisher, a New Zealand-born economist at the London Royal Institute of International Affairs, offered a classical approach to the topic of slavery and African Muslims. His writings inspired the belief that Islam itself was as guilty as the transatlantic traders. They both enforced slavery. He explained:

> In the tropical African setting, the Muslim law was not always clearly applied, and it is difficult to draw a sharp line between characteristics of African slavery, which were survivals from pre-Muslim practice, and those which were imported later with Islam.[38]

Robert Dannin, a professor of urban anthropology at New York University, titled his book *Black Pilgrimage to Islam* to express his disdain of African-American conversion/reversion to Islam. After shadowing Imam Wali Akram of the First Cleveland Mosque for weeks, he concluded:

> Conversion to Islam confronts the chronicler of African-American religion with an unusual dilemma. After digging into the past, he now finds that the present has changed, too. The paradox is that of the traveler who embarks on his long journey from an unpaved crossroads and returns to discover an international airport in its place. Meanwhile many new routes have become available, and the timetable is filled with destinations at once mysterious and unsettling in their capacity to diminish any pretensions to know the world.[39]

Some recent mainstream Muslim writers also have affiliation to this view. In her book *American Muslims: The New Generation*, Asma Gull Hasan explains, "Islam for those African-Americans during the civil rights era who chose to convert, was a means of liberation and freedom from their low status in society."[40]

The Truth Between

The disproportionately high number of African-American converts to Islam is a reality that needs an explanation. It is not only the historical consciousness that motivates these converts. By the same token, it is not an identity crisis that is bringing African-Americans to the abode of Islam. Rather, an objective and balanced reason for this phenomenon can be found in the interaction of three factors: the historical awakening, the African-American community, and the Islamic message.[41]

L's thesis on perversion

WHY MOST AMERICAN CONVERTS ARE AFRICAN-AMERICANS

The cultural philosophy of African America defines itself historically in the imaginative consciousness inherited from Africa. From the early nineteenth century to the rise of the Civil Rights Movement of 1960's, the ground of African-American intellectual discourse was neither fulfilling the American dream nor accomplishing full citizenship. Rather, the common ground was always defined dialectically to white racial ideology. As such, the further an African-American intellectual's views were from Eurocentric ideology, the more authentic and grounded they were in black cultural philosophy.

Africa, in this intellectual discourse, beautifies the idea of blackness that white racial ideology created. Anything African is defined as genuine, authentic and legitimate for black America. Therefore, if Islam is seen as partly African and historically non-European, what else is there in this exclusionary conflict that outweighs Islam as a means of identity expression in the cultural politics of difference?

A very simple anthropological explanation is that Islam, when seen as an African religion, supplies the organic solidarity between Africa and African Americans with sacred text, which is necessary in any identity linkage between individual and a central myth or entity.[42]

This legacy explains the rapid spread of the Ahmadiyyah Movement among the former Garveyites who found in Islamic identity distinctive images to express their difference in mainstream American society. The same analogy applies to the success of the Nation of Islam in attracting thousands of followers throughout the African-American community during the Civil Rights era.

This also explains why main icons of African-American cultural philosophy – Edward Wilmot Blyden (1832-1912), W. E. B. Du Bois (1868-1963), Marcus Garvey (1887-1940), and Malcolm X (1925-1965) – directly or indirectly examined Islam as a theme in the battle for cultural identity. Blyden, a Virgin Islander, traveled the African Diaspora before visiting Africa and upheld Islam in his collection of essays called *Christianity, Islam and the Negro Race*.

Du Bois, as we have seen in the previous discussion, addressed Islam as the true religion of the Negro race. Marcus Garvey closely worked with Duse Muhammad Ali (1866-1949), a Muslim Sudano-Egyptian based in London who was a pan-Islamic champion of the African and Asian independence movement of the 1920's. Garvey also invited Ahmadiyyah missionaries to his Liberty Hall headquarters in New York. The Ahmadiyyah newspaper *Sunrise* reprinted pro-Islamic articles from the *Negro World*.[43] Making Islam the official religion of Universal Negro Improvement Association (UNIA) was suggested by several delegates at the group's 1922 convention.[44] Malcolm X, whose Muslim name was Al-Haji Malik El-Shabazz, not only embraced Islam as his ideal religion, but he also established an organization called Muslim Mosques Inc. as a means of developing social programs based entirely on religious teachings.[45]

Islamic teachings and its moral order are similar to those of Christianity. They naturally appeal to all groups and classes, but mostly to those at the lower spectrum of the economic structure. Islam denies all types of segregation based on social or economic status. Although Islam encourages work ethics and wealth accumulation, it sees poverty and richness as God-given in order to test humans on matters of patience, generosity, and kindness. In addition, Islam considers what the rich give to the poor as charity a duty and never views such actions as a favor to the poor. Hence, Islam enables the poor to stand on an equal footing with the rich without feelings of inferiority based on their unfortunate material status in a moral world that does not separate religious duty and state or public and private.

In the tradition of the Prophet, known as *Athar*, Allah looks into your heart and deeds, not at your wealth and appearance. There are other *Hadiths* (Islamic traditions) from the Prophet that address the issue of poverty as a test from which come virtues of perseverance, courage, and hope.

Converts to Islam embrace the divine view that sees the material goods of life as inadequate measurement of success. They find in Islam global alternatives that are handy and within their reach. No one out there except the divine power can question each person's value and utility on this earth. As such, historically, most converts to Islam in the early days of the Prophet were the poor, the slaves, and the less noble Arab tribes.

According to the *Siratu Ibn Hisham,* which is the most classic and authentic biography of Prophet Muhammad's life (pbuh), the first believer among the men was Abu Bakar, a middle-class merchant; among the women was Khadijah, the first wife of the prophet and an upper-class businesswoman; among the youth was Ali, the prophet's nephew. After these early converts, the rest were either slaves; such as Bilal Ibn Rabah, an Abyssinian slave, and Suhaib Arroumi, a Roman slave; or they were poor Arab families, such as the Yasir family. Similar to these poor groups, were the first migrants who went to Abyssinia (modern day Ethiopia), to seek refuge due to the oppression they were facing from the upper-class Arabs of Mecca.

Mass conversion among wealthy and middle-class Arabs was a late phenomenon during the conquest of Mecca, known as *Fathu* Mecca on the twentieth *Ramadan* coinciding with January 11, 630. In the years that followed, the spread of Islam in Iraq and Egypt also started from the bottom up. In Egypt, most indigenous Christian Copts quickly converted to Islam and allied with the newcomers to oppose the church elite and the wealthy Byzantine rulers. In Iraq, the poor Bedouin Arabs readily joined the ranks of the Muslim armies against their Sassanian rulers.

More historical evidence is in the Indian subcontinent, where the spread of Islam followed, to a large extent, the demographic distribution of the lower caste people. In the Bengal region, the inhabitants, seen by high-class Hindus as slaves and unclean, readily accepted Islam at the hands of the Muslim invaders who preached that "all men are equal in the sight of Allah."[46]

In West Africa, the same attitude applied when the *Thiddo* (the lower-class peasants) in the Senegambian region accepted Islam, prompting the ruling class to follow them as a way of enforcing moral authority. In Nigeria, Islam was brought to the region by the Mandingo traders, who were known as Wangara. They spread the new religion to the lower-class farmers and slaves of Hausaland. The autocrats and landowners were the last groups to convert to Islam.[47]

The view that Islam is a religion that grows from bottom up explains why more than eighty percent of the American converts/reverts to Islam are African-Americans. Needless to say there is overwhelming evidence of economic disparity and racial biases entangling the African-American community in this country.[48]

The success of Islam in the inner city reflects another dimension of alternatives to the city inhabitants who witnessed few changes in their living conditions in the post-civil rights era. When immigrant Muslims come, as with all immigrants, American inner cities represent the starting point. African-Americans who are the primary inhabitants of the inner city, are the first to talk to them, listen to them and, in some cases, learn their ways of life. This early encounter between Muslim immigrants and African-Americans is the breeding ground of acquaintance and cultural exchange.

Many Muslim immigrants were not practicing Muslims in their homeland. But the circumstance of living in a non-Muslim society brought them to the mosque where they discovered that their cultural backgrounds were an important commodity for religious authority and leadership.

There is a common denominator that links inner-city residents and Muslim immigrants. Islam, Professor Sulayman Nyang of Howard University relates, is generally "a Third World religion."[49] The Muslim world locates largely in what are known as Third World countries. Conditions of living in most American inner cities are similar to those of the middle-class in Cairo, Islamabad, Jakarta,

Dakar, the West Bank, and Damascus. Immigrants to the United States from Third World countries are either members of the upper-class, who can afford paying tuitions at American universities, or they are middle-class workers who have the necessary connections to get a visiting or immigration visa.

Another related question is who accepts Islam among African-Americans. Milton Wilson, known as Dr. Ibrahim Abdul Akeem, an African American physician in East Cleveland, told me in an interview that conversion/reversion of the African-American middle class is "a recent phenomenon."[50] The first African-American Muslim generation consisted of people like Malcolm X and was a generation of ex-convicts, drug dealers, pimps, and those in the underground world. Walter Akim Muhammad, known as Walter Kirksey, assistant director of facilities management at the School of Medicine of Case Western Reserve University, recalled the visit of Elijah Muhammad, the spiritual leader of the Nation of Islam to Cleveland in 1958. He said Mr. Muhammad told the audience at Cory Methodist Church that "people in Cleveland are thick-headed, like a rock, hard to penetrate, but remember people in the Nation of Islam are mainly those thick-headed of the penitentiary system."[51]

Historically, the first people to provide ground to the growth of Islam in America are those described by Louis Farrakhan as the "black poor's pathology, which is product of the slavery experience."[52] Classic books of the Civil Rights era, such as Soul on Ice by Eldridge Cleaver, *Die Nigger Die* by H. Rap Brown, and *Manchild in the Promised Land* by Claude Brown, depict the ground that provided Islam with suitable elements, candidates, and dedicated followers. A neat description of this ground was detailed well in Brown's autobiography of Harlem in the 1950's and 1960's. Brown explained:

> All the time before, the junkies never had anyplace to go when he came out of jail or out of the hospital. Now the junkies had a place to go, those who could accept the teachings of the Muslims.[53]

The recent trend of conversion/reversion includes Hispanics and other marginalized minorities. According to a study by Samantha Sanchez and Juan Galvan, there are 40,000 Latino Muslims in the United States.[54]

The penitentiary system alone is producing more converts than the standing mosques. Conversion/reversion while serving jail sentence has been a legacy of heroism since the days of Malcolm X, who himself was a jail convert. Eldridge Cleaver, H. Rap Brown, and Mike Tyson followed that trend of conversion/reversion to Islam while incarcerated. In his album *Machiavelli*, the late rap star Tupac Shakur remembered his long days in jail reading the Holy Qur'an that inspired his "kicking lyrics like the Holy Qur'an."[55] According to an American Muslim Council study in 1991, about 35,000 prisoners convert to Islam each year.[56] Ramiz Islamboli who is president of Uqbah Mosque Foundation and serves as imam at the Justice Center in downtown Cleveland stated that there are more than eighty inmates who regularly attend his regular Friday sermons.[57]

As empirical evidence for the interaction of the three previously discussed factors in motivating African-American converts, let's examine some examples from the Cleveland Muslim community.

Daud Abdul Malik, imam of Masjid Al-Haqq, who is formerly known as Larry Thomas, may be the most controversial leader among the Muslim clergies of Cleveland. Known as *Diablo* (*the devil*) during the black nationalist movement of the 1970's, he converted to Islam and created the Universal Islamic Brotherhood (UIB) on the East Side of Cleveland urging Muslims of the area to migrate there and build their own community governed by internal *Sharia* code.

Imam Daud traveled the Muslim world, "observing how Muslims live and build ideal communities," he explained from his UIB headquarters. In the 1980's, he spent a few months in the *Tijaniyyah* (a *Sufi* sect) Brotherhood city of Kaolack, Senegal. This *Sufi* sect led by Sheikh Hassan Niass promotes self-reliance and discipline.

Imam Daud also traveled through the Middle East and stayed with the Muslim minority of China.

Between 1990 and 1995, Imam Daud hired seven teachers from Sudan, Zambia, Senegal, Namibia, Kenya, Somalia, and Nigeria to teach various subjects in his Islamic School of the Oasis (TISO). In his words, "I want these teachers to stop the cultural chaos of our inner-city youth."[58] In return, he sent more than twenty students overseas to study Arabic language, African history, and Islamic sciences.

When I came to this country in 1996, Imam Daud took me for a ride through the inner city. He stopped his car across from dilapidated houses at the intersection of Hayden and St. Clair avenues, observing some teenagers standing at the corner and exchanging something that I did not recognize. I understood from their unfriendly looks that they were hiding their activities from strangers and intruders like us. After a long silence behind the wheel, Imam Daud, a heavy-set man with a classic Afro that always reminds me of the famous basketball star Dr. J, exhaled his words in his thunderous voice, "Look at what they did to our people!" Because I was new in this country and had just started learning English a few months prior to my arrival, I could not figure out whom he meant by *they*.

I did not want to look stupid by asking the obvious, so I remained silent. But I was asking myself, Who are *they*? Back home in Senegal, West Africa, there is no they, only We Senegalese or others, meaning foreigners, non-Senegalese. So who are the foreigners in this land? Later, when I got to know Imam Daud and his activism, I found out who *they* are.

Imam Daud's journey to Islam explained the triangle of elements that turns in favor of Islam in the African-American journey. In his August 31, 1990 sermon at Masji Al-Haqq, he explained to his congregation:

I was a revolutionary, you understand. I wasn't scared of nothing, you understand. I tackled everything. I fought. I closed drug houses. I fought the police. I was in shootouts. I had all this stuff, but one day I woke up and I wasn't winning. Even though we closed the drug houses, our people were dying of drugs. And they liked it. They were more or less against us! So I said to myself, Well, I have to do things a little different than shooting it out with police. I am going to take eleven people that I think are abominations of evil in this world. I am going to take them out and, whatever comes, I'm going to keep fighting evil until they take me. I don't want to die without having understood the truth.[59]

Dr. Ihsan Bagby is another symbol of the triangle relationship. With a doctorate in Islamic studies, Bagby was the first African-American to become national director of education in the Islamic Society of North America. He became Muslim, following the race uprising of 1968 in Cleveland. The social unrest that followed the assassinations of Malcolm X and Dr. Martin Luther King Jr. brought thousands of youth like him to examine Islam. "I tried to be a good Christian like Dr. King but gave up when it seemed like no one else was trying," he said in an interview.[60] He converted to Islam in 1969 at Masjid Al-Mu'min, which was at Superior Avenue. In the following years, Bagby spent a year at the American University in Cairo, studying pedagogy of Islamic education. He returned to the United States to manage the board of directors of the New York based Dar al-Islam Movement. He became an active member in reforming Islamic education in North America to serve both American and immigrant Muslims.

Notes

1. Muslim writers tend to use the word revert instead of convert to connote the belief that Islam is the religion of natural inclination.

2. The difficulty in acquiring a correct estimation of the American Muslim community has several factors to it. Among them are that national census data do not reveal religious affiliation and most individual indigenous Muslims do not go by a Muslim name. Under most circumstances, African-American Muslims use two names, one in the community and another outside the community. Imam Abbas, leader of the First Cleveland Mosque, notes another factor that some Muslims are active and involved in their communities, but others are inactive.

3. See Steven Barboza, *American Jihad: Islam After Malcolm X* (New York: Doubleday, 1994), p. 15.

4. See *Council on American-Islamic Relations Report, 2002*, "The Mosque In America".

5. Some friends, as well as some of the people surveyed in this study, dismiss vehemently all explanations on the subject of conversion/reversion to Islam. They see conversion/reversion to Islam beyond the reach of social science research because, according to the Holy Qur'an (6:125), Allah is the faith giver. However, one can argue that this verse addresses the subject of faith (Iman), not Islam. In Islamic sciences, there is a difference between Islam, which is the religion, and Iman, which addresses the inner spiritual posture of a believer. All Muslims compete to reach the highest level of that spirituality.

6. For details, see Rashid Adib, *Islam, Black Nationalism, and Slavery: A Detailed History* (Maryland: Black Muslim History, 1995).

7. Sylviane Diouf, *Servants of Allah: African Muslims Enslaved in the Americas* (New York: New York University Press, 1998), p. 82.

8. Terry Alford, *Prince Among Slaves* (New York: Oxford University Press, 1977), p. 56.

9. Albert J. Raboteau, Slave Religion: The "*Invisible Institution*" *in the Antebellum South* (New York: Oxford University Press, 1978), pp 46-47.

10. Ibid, p. 47.

11. Peter H. Wood, *Black Majority* (New York: W.W. Norton & Co., 1974), p. 178.

12. J.F. Ade Ajayi and Michael Crowder, *History of West Africa* (New York: Columbia University Press, 1972), p 126.

13. Ibid, p. 155.

14. Ibid, p. 202.

15. Al-Sa'di, *Tarikh al-sudan dawn to 1613,* translated by John Hunwick under Timbuktu & the Songhay Empire (Boston: Brill, 1999), pp. 62-63.

16. These books are still widely used in rural areas of Mali, Senegal, Mauritania and Guinea.

17. Al-Sa'di, p. 54.

18. A. Adu Boahen, *African Perspectives on Colonialism* (Baltimore: The John Hopkins University Press, 1989), p. 14.

19. Nigeria is the most populous country in Africa.

20. Diouf, p. 16.

21. See Christopher Harrison, *France and Islam in West Africa,* 1860-1960 (England: Cambridge University Press, 1988), p. 107.

22. Edward W. Blyden, *Christianity, Islam and the Negro Race* (Baltimore: Black Classic Press, 1994), p. 13.

23. W. E. B. Du Bois, *Africa, Its Geography, People and Products and Africa Its Place in Modern History* (New York: KTO Press, 1977), p. 13.

24. Allan Austin, *African Muslims in Antebellum America* (New York: Gardland Publishing, 1984), p. 41.

25. Abdullah Hakim Quick, *Islam and the African in America: the Sunni Experience* (Ontario: Omni Print, 1997), p. 17.

26. Sylviane Diouf, *Servants of Allah: African Muslims Enslaved in the Americas* (New York: New York University Press, 1998).

27. Amir Nashid Ali, *Muslims In America: Seven Centuries of History* (Maryland: Amana Publication, 1998).

28. Imam Warith Deen Mohammed, *The Champion We Have In Common: The Dynamic African American Soul* (Illinois: W.D.M. Ministry Publication, 2001), p. iii.

29. Eric Lincoln "The American Muslim Mission in the Context of American Social History," *The Muslim Community in North America*, ed. Earl H. Waugh et all. (The University of Albert Press, 1983), p 224.

30. Elijah Muhammad, *Message to the Black Man* (Chicago: Muhammad Temple No.2, 1965), p. 53.

31. E.U. Essien-Udom, *Black Nationalism: A Search for an Identity in America* (Chicago: The University of Chicago Press, 1962), p. 83.

32. James Baldwin. *Notes of a Native Son* (Boston: Beacon Press, 1955), p. 45.

33. James Baldwin. *The Fire Next Time* (New York: The Dial Press, 1963), p. 95.

34. John Henrik Clarke. *Africans at the Cross Roads: Notes for an African World Revolution* (New Jersey: African World Press Inc., 1991), p. xii.

35. Chancellor Williams, *The Destruction of Black Civilization* (Chicago: Third World Press, 1987), p. 23.

36. Molefi Kete Asante, *The Afrocentric Ideas* (Philadelphia: Temple University Press, 1987), p. 182.

37. Bernard Lewis, "the African Diaspora and the Civilization of Islam." *The African Diaspora: Imperative Essays*. Edited by Maritin L. Kilson and Robert I. Rotberg. (Cambridge: Harvard University Press, 1976), p. 56.

38. Allan Fisher and Humphery Fisher, *Slavery and Muslim Society in Africa* (New York: Doubleday, 1971), p. 8.

39. Robert Dannin, *Black Pilgrimage to Islam* (New York: Oxford University Press, 2002), p. 262.

40. Asma Gull Hasan, *American Muslims: The New Generation* (New York: Continuum, 2000), p. 65.

41. Historically, the first known public convert to Islam was not an African-American. Rather, he was white, well-educated, and a career United States diplomat. Alexander Russell Webb, born in Hudson, New York, converted to Islam in 1872. Muhammad Webb his Muslim name, was appointed by President Grover Cleveland as consular of the U.S. in the Philippines in 1887. He later resigned his foreign service and spent some time touring the Muslim world. He moved back to New York where he established a

publishing company and a bookstore to propagate Islam. He represented the Muslim World at the Parliament of Religions in Chicago in 1893. (For more details on Alexander Webb, read Marc Ferris' "Immigrant Muslims in New York City," Muslim Communities in North America, edited by Yvonne Yazbeck Haddad and Janet Idleman Smith (Albany: Suny Press, 1994), p. 209.)

42. Africa is the only continent in the world where Muslims are the majority. That is why contemporary Muslims and Arab historians such as Abdul Qani Khalafallah and Hasan Ahmad Mahmud, refer to Africa as *Al-Qaratu al-Muslimah* (the Muslim Continent/ Islamic continent).

43. Yusuf Nurddidin, "African American Muslims and the Question of Identity. *Muslims on the Americanization Path?* Edited by Yvonne Yazbeck Haddad ad John L. Esposito. (New York: Oxford University Press, 2000), p. 222.

44. Martin, Op cit, p. 75.

45. See Karl Evanzz, *The Judas Factor: The Plot to Kill Malcolm X* (New York: Thunder's Mouth Press, 1992), p. 241.

46. See Jafar Sharif, *Islam in India* (New Delhi: Oriental Books Reprint Corporation, 1972), p. 8.

47. See Adam Abdullah Alluri, *Al--Islam Alyawma wa Qadan Fi-Nigerian* (Islam Today and Tomorrow in Nigeria) (Cairo: Whaba Library, 1985).

48. For instance, one-third of all young black males in their twenties are in prison, on probation, or on parole, according to Keith Richburg, *Out of America* (New York: Basic Books, 1997), p xiii. In most Uniform Crime Records, black Americans make up about fifty percent of those arrested for violent crimes. Overall, blacks, who make up twelve percent of the U.S. population, represent forty-five percent of those in prison. For more statistics on black Americans, see, for instance, *The Data Game* by Mark H. Maier. (New York: M.E. Sharpe, 1995), p. 93.

49. In Professor Nyang's introduction of Rashid Adib's book *Islam, Black Nationalism, and Slavery: A Detailed History*, Op Cit. p. 5.

50. Interviewed on October 4, 1999.

51. Interviewed on June 18, 2002.

52. Adolph Reed Jr. "The Rise of Louis Farrakhan." *The Best of the Nation.* Edited by Victor Navasky & Katrina Vanden. (New York: Nation Book, 2000), p. 96.

53. Claude Brown, *Manchild in the Promised Land* (New York: Touchstone, 1965), p. 331.

54. Samantha Sanchez and Juan Galvan, "Latino Muslims: The Changing Face of Islam in America." *Islamic Horizons* (New York: Islamic Society of North America, July/ August 2002), p. 22.

55. Conversion/reversion to Islam while serving a jail sentence is for many African-Americans a tradition that brings them closer to the legacy of Malcolm X. The fact is also that many converts go back to their old days after leaving prison, as witnessed in the reversion of Eldridge Cleaver and Mike Tyson.

56. Asma Gull Hasan, Op cit, p. 75.

57. Interviewed on December 20, 2002.

58. The statement was made during a staff meeting at The Islamic School of Oasis, November 26, 1996.

59. Dannin, Op cit, p. 251.

60. Ibid, p. 240.

Chapter 3

Genesis of Islam in Cleveland

The Real Solution to the Negro Question.

My dear American Negro, *Assalaam Alaikum*.
Peace be with you and the mercy of Allah.
The Christian profiteers brought you out of your native lands of Africa and, in Christianizing you, made you forget the religion and language of your forefathers – which were Islam – and [the Christian religion] proved to be no good. It is a failure. Christianity cannot bring real brotherhood to nations. So, now leave it alone.
And join Islam, the real faith of Universal Brotherhood.

[*The Moslem Sunrise*, April and July, Vol. 2, 1923, Chicago]

Until now, there has not been a comprehensive study about Islam in Cleveland. Literature concerning the history of Islam in Cleveland can be categorized into three groups:

1. Fragmentary information found in newspaper reports, notably in the *Cleveland Press, Call and Post* and *The Plain Dealer*. Most of these reports need to be cross-examined, and compared with other sources in order to provide clear-cut primary source documents for historical research.

2. Mosques and community archives, especially those of the First Cleveland Mosque, which offers a substantial reference concerning Islam in Cleveland. Imam Wali Abdul Akram, leader of the community, operated a printing house inside the mosque where he filed the Ahmaddiyah documents of the First Cleveland Mosque activities. The archive of the mosque is not classified, nor is it organized to be accessible to researchers. Some documents are scattered within the mosque building, while others are in personal possession of the Akram family. These documents contain a variety of newspaper articles, pictures, correspondences, and early publications about Islam in Cleveland and Northeast Ohio.

3. Oral history, which remains the main source for studying Islam in Cleveland. These memories range from the experiences of those imams and sheikhs who organized communities as individuals converted to Islam, and the tales of the early Muslim immigrants who strived to establish mosques and communities of believers. Throughout the eleven main Muslim communities, most founding members are still alive and their accounts and stories provide the backbone of this study.

The Ahmadiyyah Movement

The Ahmaddiyah movement, founded in India in the last decade of the nineteenth century and led by Mirza Ghulam Ahmad, was the most active movement in proselytizing Islam in the modern world.[1] It is considered heretical for its claims of prophethood in the person of its founder, thus breaking one of the most sacred Islamic beliefs in which Prophet Muhammad is the last messenger of Allah.

Consequently, the Ahmaddiyah is banned in most of the traditional Muslim world, and its followers are expelled from the community of Islam throughout the Muslim world.[2]

However, the Ahmadiyyah was the first Muslim organization to engage in literary activities with other religious groups, especially those outside the traditionally Muslim world. For instance, in 1897, the movement established its first Urdu weekly periodical *al-Hakam*. In 1902, it created *al-Badar*, which was a monthly publication in English. In the same year, it also started a remarkable and regular publication titled *The Review of Religions*, which became over the years the single organ of propagating Islam in the English-speaking world.[3] By the turn of the twentieth century, Ahmadiyyah followers started providing Islamic literature in English and successfully established themselves in England. One of the Ahmadiyyah's main figures, Mawlana Muhammad Ali, offered the first English version of the Holy Qur'an that was accepted throughout the world.

In the United States, the first Ahmadiyyah missionary arrived in Chicago in 1920. Mufti Muhammad Sadiq, who was from northern India, now Pakistan, established the Ahmadiyyah Mosque and extended the movement's membership offices into major cities of North America. By 1923, he had developed close ties with Marcus Garvey's Universal Negro Improvement Association.[4] Although the movement did not manifest racial preferences in its activities, in the United States, the African-American community represented the bulk of the movement's activities. From Chicago, followers distributed the Qur'an in its English translation. In 1921, they started providing copies of the journal *The Review of Religions* and created the first Muslim newspaper in the United States, the *Moslem Sunrise*.

Furthermore, the Ahmadiyyah provided the translation of the primary sources of Islamic scholarship, such as *Hadith* and commentary of *Bukhari*, and commentary of *Muslim*. Thus, the movement was the first to expose mainstream Americans to the literature and teachings of Islam.[5] Ahmadiyyah provided the essence of Islamic literature to the American Muslim community for many decades. This movement represents the oldest Muslim movement to successfully reach the African-American masses beginning with its Islamic message in the early 1920s. Most pioneers of African-American Islamic organizations, such as Timothy Drew Ali, founder of the Moorish Science Temple, Fard Muhammad, the spiritual founder of the Nation of Islam, and Imam Wali Akram, founder of the Moslim Ten Year Plan in Cleveland, were directly influenced by the philosophy and teachings of the Ahmadiyyah missionaries. After infertile efforts to convert white Americans, the movement concentrated its efforts on the African-American community and successfully converted Garveyites and black nationalists. This Ahmadiyyah movement established the first Islamic missionaries who influenced the African-American community in Cleveland.

In 1930, the Ahmadiyyah movement officially opened the First Cleveland Mosque office space at Woodland Avenue; the temporary meeting place was at 2226 E. 55th Street.[6] The head of this local branch was an Indian missionary called Abul M. Fazl, a representative of *Sufi* M. R. Bengalee in Chicago, who became head of the Ahmadiyyah movement in America.[7]

The movement's approach to proselytizing Islam was to send missionaries and newly converted Muslims to propagate the religion throughout the city. They stopped people on the street at clubs and in public parks. They even went house to house to introduce residents to the teachings of Islam.

African-Americans formed most of the membership of the movement while all the missionaries were from the Indian subcontinent. The Cleveland missionaries were offering evening classes in the Woodland *Masjid* (mosque). These daily classes focused on Islamic and Arabic studies, the Qur'an and *Hadith* (the tradition of the Prophet Muhammad). There were weekly meetings in the *Masjid*, which were well-supplied with Ahmadiyyah publications including the *Moslem Sunrise, The Review of Religions*, and the Qur'an and its commentary. Members who graduated from these meetings were named Sheikh, an Arabic word that identified them as having adequate Islamic knowledge to be leaders.

By 1930, there were fifty Sheikhs throughout the United States. One of the early Americans to be promoted to this title was Wali Abdul Akram, a resident of Cleveland and a member of the First Mosque at Woodland Avenue.

Akram was born Walter R. Gregg on August 4, 1904, in Caldwell, Texas. He entered Prairie View State College at age of fourteen. Prairie View was a vocational land-grant college of the Tuskegee training method. Walter Gregg was able to work his way through studying electrical engineering. In 1924, he decided to go to St. Louis "to experience some of the things that he had read about Islam," to quote his older son's words.[8] On this journey, he met sheikh Ahmad Din, one of the earlier Ahmadiyyah recruited in America and considered the first person in the country to be nominated Sheikh. Ahmad

Din urged Gregg to "get back your language and your religion, and you won't be a Negro anymore."[9]

After his conversion/reversion to Islam,[10] Wali Akram headed north accompanied by his converted wife, Kareemah. They followed the Ahmadiyyah missionaries in the Midwest cities of Cincinnati, Pittsburgh, and Cleveland. "They worked hard taking Islam to Southern migrants, who shared similar backgrounds and had been enticed to the north by the myth of prosperity."[11] The young Wali Akram found Cleveland attractive with approximately 300 Ahmadiyyah followers.[12]

In 1934, the new Ahmadiyyah representative in the United States, *Sufi* M. Yusuf Khan of India, was spending most of his time in the Cleveland branch, instead of the headquarters in Chicago. The Ahmadiyyah community was totally dependent on instructions from the movement leadership in India. Furthermore, the decision-making circle in Cleveland was totally foreign. Although Wali Akram was not responsible at the organizational level, he was active in the community and was the only African-American sheikh in the movement. His name was signed to several significant pieces of correspondence that indicated his authority. He was the mastermind behind the eighteen African-Americans who, in 1935, signed the petition in Judge Brewer's courtroom to change their names.[13]

But his relationship with the Ahmadiyyah Movement soon deteriorated. The account of the story was documented as follows: In 1937, *Sufi* Bengalee, the newly appointed chair of the Chicago headquarters, who was at this time directly supervising the activities of the movement in Cleveland, returned to the headquarters in India. Wali Akram, with a group of other African-American Muslims, created an organization called the Moslem Ten Year Plan (MTYP).[14] The goal of this group was to respond to the economic needs of the African-American members of the movement. Wali Akram, without permission, added the MTYP to the Ahmadiyyah official letterhead and started sending it out to UNIA Hall on Euclid Avenue to recruit members for the organization.

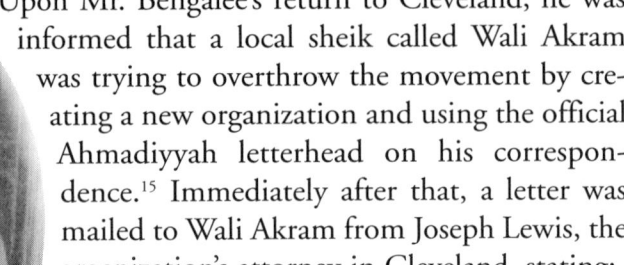

Wali Abdul Akram in 1937. Akram transformed the First Cleveland Mosque into an orthodox mosque.

Upon Mr. Bengalee's return to Cleveland, he was informed that a local sheik called Wali Akram was trying to overthrow the movement by creating a new organization and using the official Ahmadiyyah letterhead on his correspondence.[15] Immediately after that, a letter was mailed to Wali Akram from Joseph Lewis, the organization's attorney in Cleveland, stating:

Sufi M. R. Bengalee, M.A, the head of the Ahmadiyyah Movement in Islam in the United States of America, has consulted me with regard to your activities. He has requested me to write you requiring that you cease upon receipt of this letter, from using the name of the movement in any connection whatsoever with any of your activities. By February 10th, 1937, if the sign is not removed from your meeting place and the name of the movement removed from your literature, identification cards, and any circulation distributed by you, I have been instructed by court proceeding to effectuate this. In the future, you are not to use the name "the Ahmadiyyah Movement in Islam" in any manner, in your activities.[16]

Upon receiving this letter, Imam Wali Akram was forced to leave the Ahmadiyyah Movement to start fully working in the name of the MTYP. He had already become acquainted with *Sunni* Islam through his association with a small Muslim group made

Mosque of the Ahmadiyyah Muslim Community Cleveland Chapter. Now located at Bedford Heights. President: Nazim Rehmatullah (Mainstream Muslims have denounced the Ahmadiyyah beliefs as deviation from the true teachings of Islam.)

up of Turks, Syrians, and other Muslim immigrants who used to conduct Friday prayers in their private homes.[17] Therefore, *Sunni* Islam, Islamic orthodoxy was the chosen philosophy for the MTYP group who retained the name of the First Cleveland Mosque for their meeting place at 7605 Woodland after their departure from the Ahmadiyyah. Most of the local Muslim community sided with the newly established MTYP. The Ahmadiyyah Movement, after losing one of its main propagators, reduced its missionary presence in Cleveland and slowly shifted its focuses to Pittsburgh, Pennsylvania.

The First Cleveland Mosque and the MTYP

Imam Wali Akram quickly drafted a regional plan for the newly formed Moslem Ten Year Plan. The first phase of its agenda was the domain of economic empowerment of the Muslim communities. The aims of the organization was to "provide for the absolute necessities of life and to spread the practical benefits of the humanistic ideas of Islam."[18] In 1937, the MTYP was chartered as a not-for-profit organization and Imam Akram was nominated its president. The next year, Akram started an ambitious plan of creating a national organization to unify all Muslims scattered throughout the country. In a quest to establish a national Muslim organization, Akram invited all Islamic orthodox groups in the country to a national convention of unity. The four main orthodox groups in the country at that time attended the convention in Philadelphia on August 18, 1943. They were Adenu Allahe Universal Arabic Association (AAUAA) headed by Professor Muhammad Ezaldeen in Philadelphia and Newark; Harlem Academy of Islam led by Sheikh Omar Ali of Harlem; Moslems of America leaded by Sheikh Nasir Ahmad of Pittsburgh, and the MTYP.[19]

The convention lasted four days and, on the final day, the attendees visited AAUAA's resettlement farms in nearby New Jersey. During the meetings, a national body was crafted under the name of United Islamic Society of America (UISA). Wali Abdul Akram was unanimously elected president.

Back in Cleveland, Wali Akram devoted his time to spreading orthodox Islam among the rising waves of black nationalism. On the one hand, he extended the sphere of the MTYP. He established branches in several Ohio cities – notably Youngstown, Akron, Cincinnati, and Dayton – to foster development and the educational role of the Muslim communities. On the other hand, he suggested to the membership of UISA that the group adopt a more conciliatory and tolerant brand of Islam. In the second national convention of UISA, he enfranchised women members of the organization by appointing two women delegates from the Muslim League of Islamic Brotherhood in St. Louis to the constitutional subcommittee.

Unlike other Muslim leaders and black nationalist groups such as the Nation of Islam, who discouraged their members from participating in World War II, Akram did not object to members of Muslim organizations joining the Army to show their patriotic duty during the war. He also invited non-

Imam Wali Akram is shown in front of the MTYP headquarters in Cleveland in this 1950 photograph. The writing in the background is "Moslem Ten Year Plan, a religious, industrial, and economical organization for the service of humanity."

This 1945 photograph taken at the First Cleveland Mosque shows women members of the Moslem Ten Year Plan.

Muslims to join the MTYP as way of forging a larger community. The MTYP also established a burial fund for the Muslim community and an educational center to fill the vacuum left by the Ahmadiyyah's withdrawal from the area.[20]

In 1945, a regional convention of Muslim organization was held in Cleveland and the Cleveland Herald newspaper made that event a front-page story.[21]

With the rise of the Nation of Islam and the civil rights movement, most of the regional branches of the UISA shifted to local focus, thus diminishing the regional influence of the MTYP. Imam Wali Akram (seated in the front row in white turban) also found his effort to structure the UISA worthless with the rise of traditionalist and separatist approaches that envisaged boycotting the mainstream American way of life, and encouraged Muslims to abandon political organizations.

By 1954, Imam Wali Akram had shifted his focus locally to the First Cleveland Mosque. He became the only orthodox imam of the Muslim community of Cleveland. Those who did not know him called him "Reverend" while his followers, who were estimated at 1,000 called him "Imam." He carried on his shoulders the responsibility of disentangling the false teachings of the Nation of Islam by preaching harmony and tolerance among his followers. His views were captured in this 1954 article in the Cleveland *Call & Post*, in which he was asked how many Negroes were included in the 1,000 members of the First Cleveland Mosque? Imam Akram succinctly replied, "How can we answer that when we have no Negro Muslim and White Muslims? We have Muslims and they are equal. All men are the same."[22] Akram's followers spearheaded the blossoming of mosques in Cleveland.

In 1957, Imam Wali Akram left the country with a *Jamat at-tabliq* group[23] to teach Islam around the world. In this journey that lasted a year and a half, Akram, with three friends from Pakistan, toured England, Greece, Yugoslavia, Turkey, Saudi Arabia, Pakistan, and India. His diary reveals his intention to document the journey in a manuscript titled "From the Cotton Fields of the South to the Sandy Deserts of Arabia." He wrote in his journal:

> I decided that a book should be published explaining and exemplifying facts as to the many experiences witnessed, so as not to persuade or emotionalize anyone, nor create a spirit of hatred. But simple facts that would stimulate a close relationship between the East and the West and thus help to bring peace and tranquility to people throughout the world.

This diary reflects the human side of Wali Akram, who portrays his pilgrimage as similar to mankind's journey in this world:

> We are all travelers and pilgrims in this world from birth to death. And at death our journey is ended; all variances and differences in this world are cancelled by death. With this end in view, my mission was to make pilgrimage to Mecca and have a personal observation of higher spiritual existence.

Unfortunately, most of the papers are missing and the available portion of this journal only covers his European experience.

In Belgrade, Yugoslavia, Akram recounts the unfamiliarity of his group with this homogeneous society:

> There was no English speaking people to be seen, and we were to [the] attraction of the city as though we were aliens. Finally, one man said "Muslims" and then smiles began to appear on our faces.

The divested post-World War II economy in Europe also appeared in Akram's diary as he traveled across central Europe by train.

> The sights I saw were horrible -1st, 2nd, and 3rd class waiting rooms occupied by old, young, babies, men and women all rushing to go somewhere. Their luggage was old boxes, gunny sacks filled with stale bread, now and then a suitcase.

In the Balkans and Greece, Akram wrote:

> The masses seemly, are illiterate and very backwards. Most were immigrating to their homeland – Greece or Turkey. We were the darkest people that had been seen since we left England.

Akram painted a detailed picture of people he met in his journey: young, old, male and female. On his way through Greece, he wrote:

> We arrive in Salonika (Thessolonike) [Thessalonica], Greece on May 29th at 9:30 am. Some place before we reached the borders of Greece, families with little children boarded the train with babies crying as though they were in pain and agony, some sick, ragged. When food was given by the mother it was gunny black, rye bread, a hunk of strong cheese and a tin cup of water. The food was carried in a gunny sack and it could be smelled all over the train.

In some circumstances, Akram shared his feelings toward poor and depraved families whom he met in his journey. In his way to Greece, he wrote:

> There was no place for these people to sit so the mother, father and all of these little ones were herded in the isle (which is on one side of each) as though they were animals. [I] tried to sleep, [but] I had to give up my seat; my conscience would not leave me alone…I can to this day hear the screaming of little babies crying for food and water and [I] don't think they know what milk is. I gave them my reserved seat, along with two others I stood up and slept until we reached our next stop.

In Turkey, Akram demonstrated his knowledge of history, art, and the Ottoman Empire. He gave a scrupulous description of main mosques, their architects and the Ottoman Sultan's motivation for building them.

Imam Akram's diary reflects his humanistic views on human nature as good and peaceful. If the rest of this historical piece is found, it would constitute the core of his biography.[24] Upon his arrival in Mecca, Akram was identified by Saudi Arabian officials as the second American citizen to have completed the pilgrimage in the Holy Land.[25]

In the following years, Akram revisited Mecca in 1978 and in 1986. He toured academic institutions of Northeast Ohio lecturing on theology classes and Islamic history. In the meantime, he served as chairman of community relations Board of the Muslim Student Association of North America. He was also appointed to the Cleveland Community Relations Board.

Between 1960 and 1994, the year of Akram's death, the rise of black nationalism and social unrest that followed the civil rights movement did not overshadow his message which made the First Cleveland Mosque the milestone of peace-making among the diverse religious groups of Greater Cleveland. Most importantly, Akram's orthodox approach to Islam stirred the creation of additional orthodox mosques and Muslim communities in the Cleveland area. Muslim immigrants passed through the door of the First Cleveland Mosque to establish Islamic centers and mosques. Furthermore, Masjid Al-Mumin, Masjid An-Nur and Masjid Ummatullah, which are three prominent orthodox mosques in the African-American neighborhoods of Cleveland, were founded by Akram's former associates.

Masjid Al-Mu'min

In 1953 Afzal Nabi, a friend of Imam Wali Akram and a founding member of MTYP, foresaw the importance of creating a mosque in the heart of the black nationalist groups. He chose the corner of 125th Street on Superior Avenue and established Al-Mumin Mosque (Masjid Al-Mu'min). In 1969, when brother Abdul Bashir -Udeen, stepped down as acting Imam, Mutawaf Abdus-Shaheed, a young, black nationalist who moved from New York to Cleveland, took over the leadership. Masjid Al-Mu'min became known as Islamic Revival Movement (IRM). Under Imam Mutawaf, who is nowadays the longest serving imam in Cleveland, Masjid Al-Mumin joined the alliance of the national Darul-Islam movement, which is a national organization that preaches the Islamic philosophy of Malcolm X.

Masjid An-Nur

This masjid is another offspring of the First Cleveland Mosque. In 1974, a group of Muslims who were affiliated with the *Jamat at-tabliq* of India preferred to establish a mosque where foreign missionaries could stay during their visits to Greater Cleveland. Omar Samiullah and Ali Abdullah, two trustees of the newly formed group, purchased a duplex on East 99th Street and transformed it into Masjid An-Nur. Samiullah, who accepted Islam through Imam Wali Akram, was previously active with the First Cleveland Mosque.[26] Muhammad Yunus Ali, a native of India who came to Cleveland in 1973, was frequenting the First Cleveland Mosque where he found out about the newly established mosque. The group appointed him imam of the mosque, a role he continues in now nearly 30 years late.[27]

Masjid Ummatullah

This masjid was founded in 1978 at East 83rd Street and Quincy Avenue by Imam Abdul Muqtadir Ghandi. Ghandi moved from New Jersey to Cleveland with the already established Allah's Community Mosque. In the following year, Sulayman Abdul Malik, a native of Cleveland and a former associate of Wali Akram and the First Cleveland Mosque, replaced Ghandi and since then has become the acting imam of this community.

Ummatullah's community has adopted strict interpretation of Islamic teachings. Abdul Malick describes the community's teachings as:

> Pure Islam that reflects the *Sunnah* [path] of the Prophet (pbuh). Our women cover themselves according to the Islamic teachings. We don't impose it on them; it is their own choice.[28]

This small community does not permit intermingling of sexes. Most female members wear a *Nikhab* (veil), according to the imam.

Imam Warith Deen Muhammad, known as American Muslim spokesman, led the Friday preyer at Zelma Watson George Community Center. The July 19, 2002 event commemorated the 65th anniversary of Imam Wali Akram and the establishment of the First Cleveland Mosque.

The outstanding legacy of Imam Wali Abdul Akram in preaching the Islamic message of peace and love was echoed by speakers and participants in the 65th anniversary celebration of the First Cleveland Mosque. On July 19, 2002, Mayor Jane Campbell of Cleveland and Ward 3 Councilman Zachary Reed arranged to rename Lambert Street off East 131st Street in honor of Imam Wali Akram, a man who had spent more than seven decades of his life spreading the Islamic message of peace, love, and unity.

Notes

1. The history of this movement is quite interesting. Because birth records were not kept during this time, the probable date of Mirza Ahmad's birth was February 13,1835. The turning point in his life was the year 1880 when he started publishing the four-volume *Magnum Opus, the Barahin*, which was translated as *Proofs of the Ahmadiyyah*. These publications established the reputation of his movement throughout the Indian subcontinent. One of Ahmad's controversial statements in his writings was his explanation of the Islamic term *Jihad*, which means, literally, struggling in the way of Allah. Ahmad suggested a new interpretation that would link *Jihad* with *Tabliq*, which became known among his followers as missionary in the cause of Allah. Four years later, he translated his philosophy into action by claiming to be the promised *messiah* and messenger of all nations. According to his account, he received divine commands appointing him as *mujaddid*, or renewer of the Muslim faith, that Allah had recommended him to create a new community based on making *Bay'ah*, or allegiance, to his teachings. He, therefore, recommended his followers to observe six rules:

– Abstain from associating something with God.
– Perform *Salat*, five-prayers daily.
– Remain Faithful to God and His messenger.
– Obey the teachings of the Qur'an.
– Obey the teachings of the Prophet Muhammad (pbuh).
– Obey a brotherhood with Ahmad in obedience and become a missionary in the cause of Islam.

This last point constitutes the core of the Ahmadiyyah's success in the West. The movement, by exchanging the notion of *Jihad* with missionary duty, and by adopting allegiance to the cause of Islam, became the first Muslim organization to establish its message beyond the traditional boundaries of the Muslim World. See: Harza Mirza, *Ahmadiyyah Movement: A History and Perspective* (New Delhi: Monahar Book Services, 1974).

2. For instance, in 1974 the Pakistani Council of *Ulama* declared the Ahmadiyyah Movement to be heretical.

3. See Ghulam Ahmad's writings in Yohanan Friedmann's *Prophecy Continuous* (California: The University of California Press, 1989), p. 11.

4. Tony Martin, *Race First: The Ideological and Organizational Struggles of Marcus Garvey and the Universal Negro Improvement Association* (Westport: Green Wood Press, 1976), pp. 75-77.

5. See, for example, Aminah Beverly McCloud, *African American Islam* (New York: Routledge, 1995), p. 18.

6. Throughout the United States, the name "First Mosque" symbolizes the legacy of the Ahmadiyyah Movement. Earlier mosques were called First Mosque, as they were the spearheads in establishing mosques in U.S. They were thus named in recognition that the group had spearheaded establishing mosques in this country.

7. The First Cleveland Mosque archive, Ahmadiyyah Movement pamphlet, 1930.

8. Interview with Mahmud Akram on March 5, 1999. Also see, The First Cleveland Mosque & Cuyahoga Community College, *Grand Feast to Honor Al-Haji Wali Akram.* Ed. First Cleveland Mosque, June 5, 1983.

9. Robert Dannin, *Black Pilgrimage to Islam* (New York: Oxford University Press, 2002), p. 37.

10. According to Imam Abbas, grandson and current imam of the First Cleveland Mosque, Wali Akram heard a speaker asking him if he wanted to be free. When he said, "Yes, I want to be free," the speaker said, "So you have to change your name; freedom starts from liberating yourself from that slave name." From this point, Walter Gregg became Wali Abdul Akram. He then joined the group as a Moorish Drew Ali follower, a black national Muslim movement that affiliated with the Moor culture of North Africa. (Interviewed on January 16, 1999.)

11. Ahmad Hussein, "Al-Haji Wali Akram: 1937-1952." Presented at the 65th *Anniversary of the First Cleveland Mosque* (First Cleveland Mosque, July 25, 2002).

12. Robert Dannin, *Black Pilgrimage to Islam* (New York: Oxford University Press, 2002), p. 38.

13. See Wali Akram's correspondence with Cleveland Board of Elections. Letter addressed to Mr. Louis Simon on May 26, 1935. The First Cleveland Mosque, MTYP File.

14. The First Cleveland Mosque Archive. MTYP Meeting, p. 3

15. Wali Akram, MTYP File, the First Cleveland Mosque archive.

16. Letter signed by Joseph M. Lewis, lawyer, 705 Guarantee Title Building, Cleveland, February 6, 1937. The First Cleveland Mosque, MTYP File.

17. Ahmad Hussein, Op. cit., p. 2

18. "Imam of Moslems has 10-Year Plan." *The Cleveland Plain Dealer,* (June 20, 1937).

19. Robert Dannin, *Black Pilgrimage to Islam* (New York: Oxford University Press, 2002), p. 48.

20. See *The Moslem Ten Year Plan File* at the First Cleveland Mosque archive.

21. *The Cleveland Herald,* (January 19, 1945).

22. *Call & Post,* (March 13,1954).

23. *Jamat al-Tabliq* group considers *Tabliq* (propagation) more important than most Islamic rituals. As such, they organize Muslims from diverse backgrounds and countries to travel for specified time to promote Islam and foster multicultural relationships between Muslims.

24. I got a copy of the diary from Mahmud Akram, Imam Wali Akram's oldest son.

25. *The Plain Dealer* (August 3, 1994).

26. Interviewed on January 28, 2003.

27. Email interview on February 14, 2003.

28. Phone Interview with Imam Sulayman Abdul Malik on, May 16, 2002.

Chapter 4

The Muslim Experience of Black Americans

> Ever notice the growing number of bright-red fezzes
> among the rest of the headgear on the Central Area and
> Glenville streets? They're not Elks on parade. They're members
> of Cleveland's Moslem movement, a group that is growing so rapidly
> that there are now 1,000 members in this area,
> with more added to the rolls weekly.
>
> [*Call & Post*, March 13, 1954]

Black Muslim Activism

Social uprising in the United States during the 1960's had a tremendous impact on the rise of Islam in the African-American community. The civil rights movement, in its moderation, was mostly influenced by the Southern Christian Leadership Conference. But the civil rights movement in its extreme form was mostly influenced by the Nation of Islam.[1] In other words, Martin Luther King Jr. represented a non-violent approach from a Christian organization viewpoint, but Malcolm X (or Al-Haji Malik El-Shabbaz, his Muslim name) represented a retaliatory approach from a Muslim organization viewpoint.

Malcolm X, according to several historians, was one of the most influential African-American leaders in modern history.[2] His religious image was juxtaposed with his social and political message; hence, he attracted attention to his political goals as well as to his religious message.

Claude Brown's autobiography, which depicts the everyday life of blacks in Northern ghettoes, especially in Harlem, in the 1950's and 1960's, catches the black Muslim influence on the civil rights movement. "The Muslims were the home team," Brown wrote. "They were the people talking for everyone. This was the first time that many of these people had ever seen the home boys get up and say anything in front of a crowd."[3]

Elijah Muhammad, the supreme leader of the Nation of Islam, saw his organization's message to be the sole solution for blacks in the United States. As such, he appealed to the black masses to join his ranks and contest discrimination and racism in American society. In due course, Islam became a social phenomenon among African American leaders.

Following his separation from the Nation of Islam, Malcolm X started his own branch of orthodox Islam by creating two institutions: Muslim Mosque Inc. and Organization for Afro-American Unity (OAAU). The former was dedicated to religious purposes, and the latter furthered his political message.[4]

During the 1960's the great heavyweight-boxing champion Muhammad Ali symbolized the black Muslim social rebellion. He readily displayed his affiliation with the Nation of Islam. For instance, in the 1965 buildup to fight Floyd Patterson, a Roman Catholic heavyweight, Patterson declared, "The black Muslim influence must be removed from boxing." When Ali won the fight, he was depicted as a revolutionary Muslim.[5]

September 7, 1966: Muhammad Ali kneels with other Muslims in Frankfurt, West Germany's only mosque. The world heavyweight-boxing champion played a dynamic role in popularizing Islam in the 1960's.

[Picture courtesy: Cleveland Public Library]

In the early 1970's, Lewis Alcindor, a rising basketball star who would six times be named the NBA's most valuable player, became a devoted Muslim and changed his name to Kareem Abdul-Jabbar. Like Ali, he played a role in popularizing Islam in the mainstream culture.[6]

This same decade witnessed a mass trend among African-American artists and prisoners to adopt the religion of Islam as a part of following the legacy of the slain Muslim and civil rights leader Malcolm X. For example, LeRoi Jones, a leader and founder of the Black Arts School in Harlem, became Muslim and adopted the name Amiri Baraka. Nationally renowned poet Rolland Snellings also converted to Islam and took the name Askia Muhammad Toure. Toure extensively adopted metaphorical style to express his Islamic beliefs and spiritual attachment to the legacy of Malcolm X. He attracted students of black studies and African-American studies with his allusions to Islam.[7]

In the other hand, Islam became the main source of pride and black nationalism among incarcerated African-Americans. Claude Brown describes this phenomenon in his 1965 book:

> It seems as though over the next few years, say from 1955 through 1959, just about everybody who came out of jail came out a Muslim. By 1959, I had come to the conclusion that few Negroes could go to any of the city prisons in New York and not come out a Muslim.[8]

For instance, H. Rap Brown, former minister of justice of the Black Panther Party, represents a dynamic example of this conversion in the prison system. In 1967, he declared to a civil right rally in Cambridge, Maryland, "It's time for Cambridge to explode, baby. Black folks built America, and if America doesn't come around, we're going to burn America down. I say violence is necessary. It is as American as cherry pie."[9] He then converted to Islam while serving five years in prison after a shootout with New York police. After his jail term, he moved to Atlanta's West End, where he established a nationwide Muslim community. Brown, who is known as Imam Jamil Abdullah Al-Amin, established one of the largest Muslim communities in the United States, the *National Ummah* with more than thirty-six mosques around the country. Imam Al-Amin is now serving a prison term for the alleged killing of a police officer in Atlanta.

Another controversial figure in the circle of conversion/reversion to Islam is Eldridge Cleaver former minister of information in the Black Panther Party and author of *Soul on Ice*, one of the classic works of the civil rights movement. He converted to Islam while serving time in the San Quentin prison in Los Angeles. Ironically, Cleaver also became a born-again Christian after his return from nine-year exile in France, 1976.[11]

Under these circumstances, Islam was no longer merely a religious conviction, but rather it had become a social and political platform that some African-Americans adopted in their struggle for social justice.

Black Nationalism and Islam in Cleveland

In Cleveland, adopting the Muslim platform became de facto among African-American militant groups. The 1960's black boycott against McDonald's fast food restaurant on 105th Street and Superior Avenue because it refused to franchise to black businessmen revealed the extent of Muslim influence in African-American activism. Tariq Salim Ziyad recounts that, among the twenty-one black organizations constituting the alliance for this boycott, the only literature always available in the meeting room was the Nation of Islam newspaper, *Muhammad Speaks*.[12] Throughout the protests, *Muhammad Speaks* was quoted and brandished as the official journal of the militant speakers.[13] Eventually, the newspaper, which was launched in 1962, became the largest minority weekly publication in the country. It reached more than 600,000 readers under Malcolm X's editorial leadership.[14]

This sense of activism among the members of Cleveland's black community led Martin Luther King Jr., at the peak of the civil rights movement, to declare Cleveland would be a "target city" for the Southern Christian Leadership Conference.[15] Malcolm X considered Cleveland a city where the angry mass had to be mobilized for the cause of black activism. He observed, "Black social dynamite is in Cleveland, Philadelphia, San Francisco, Los Angeles. The black man's anger is there, fermenting."[16]

On April 3, 1964, Malcolm X gave his famous speech, "The Ballot or the Bullet," at the Cory Methodist Church in Cleveland. The meeting, which was sponsored by the Cleveland Chapter of the Congress of Racial Equality (CORE), took the form of a symposium titled "The Negro Revolt --What Comes Next?"

On the eve of the symposium, Lomax told the crowd, "I am convinced that Malcolm X is a man that cannot be ignored. Instead of attempting to hide him under our wall to wall morality, let's bring him out into the open and say Brother Malcolm, on this I disagree, and let's debate the issue like honorable men." (*The Call & Post*, April 11, 1964).

In this historic speech that was repeated on several occasions throughout 1964, Malcolm X laid down two characteristics that remain fundamental in the formation of African-American Muslim communities.

Malcolm X chatting with Louis Lomax before their impressionable speeches at the Cory Methodic Church of Cleveland, April 3, 1964
Picture courtesy:
Western Reserve Historical Society

First, unlike the non-engagement in politics espoused by his former organization, the Nation of Islam, Malcolm X suggested that American Muslims should engage in political activism but not allow Islam to separate them from other Americans concerned with justice, equality and civil rights. He explained:

> I would like to say, in closing, a few things concerning the Muslim Mosque Inc., which we established recently in New York City. It's true we're Muslims and our religion is Islam, but we don't mix our religion with our politics and our economics and our social and civil activities, not any more. We keep our religion in our mosque. After our religious services are over, then as Muslims we become involved in political action, economic action, and social and civic action. We become involved with anybody, anywhere, any time and in any manner that's designed to eliminate the evils – the political, economic and social evils that are afflicting the people of our community.

Second, black nationalism was the formal ideology of his political philosophy. He urged black neighborhoods to seize ownership of their issues:

> The political philosophy of black nationalism means that the black man should control the politics and the politicians in his own community; no more. The black man in the black community has to be re-educated into the science of politics so he will know what politics is supposed to bring him in return. Don't be throwing out any ballots. A ballot is like a bullet. You don't throw your ballots until you see a target, and if that target is not within your reach, keep your ballot in your pocket.

The speech became the most characteristic of Malcolm X's visions on black nationalism, in clear opposition to Dr. King's non-violent views. Malcolm X's approach was "whatever means necessary" to achieve social, economic, and political equality in America.

About 3,000 people attended the Cory symposium.[17] They included civil right activists, Muslims, young urban blacks and many whites.

Malcolm X addressing a crowd of 3,000 at the
Cory Methodist Church in Cleveland, April 3, 1964

He made it clear that:

"I'm still a Muslim, my religion is still Islam. That's my personal belief. Just as Adam Clayton Powell is a Christian minister who heads the Abyssinian Baptist Church in New York, but at the same time takes part in the political struggles to try and bring about rights to the black people in this country; and Dr. Martin Luther King is a Christian minister down in Atlanta, Georgia, who heads another organization fighting for the civil rights of black people in this country; and Rev. Galamison – I guess you've heard of him -- is another Christian minister in New York who has been deeply involved in the school boycotts to eliminate segregated education; well, I myself, am a minister, not a Christian minister, but a Muslim minister and I believe in action on all fronts by whatever means necessary."[18]

[Picture courtesy: Western Reserve Historical Society]

In answering the question, "What next in the Negro revolt?" Author Louis Lomax called for economic integration, which he considered to be the most urgent need for blacks in America, but Malcolm X explained to Clevelanders that what was coming next would be either the ballot or the bullet.[19]

Malcolm X's speech inspired the next civil rights activist generation, as well as the rise of Muslims in black communities throughout the country. In 1969, Malcolm X's philosophy inspired Stokely Carmichael, Eldridge Cleaver, and Huey P. Newton to establish the national Black Panther Party.

The 1968 nationally reported uprising in Cleveland's Glenville neighborhood represented the extent to which some black nationalist Muslim groups misinterpreted Malcolm X's philosophy of resistance. The leaders in the shoot-out were mostly black Muslims. Fred Evans, better known as Ahmad, the top organizer of the riot, had attended Masjid Al-Mumin on Superior Avenue. Evans was later sentenced to death for his role in the bloody shootout with the police that took many lives and destroyed the economic infrastructure of the neighborhood. Before the riot, Ahmed Evans had indulged in prophecy in March 1967, creating the Black Movement of New Libya.

Fred "Ahmad" Evans, a former attendee of Masjid Al-Mumin at Superior Avenue and founder of New Libya, was charged with leading the attack that started the Glenville Riot. He was found guilty of first-degree murder and sentenced to death on May 12, 1969.

[Picture courtesy: Black Study Department at Cleveland State University]

In Muslim popular culture, Libya is perceived as one of the cradles of uprisings during the nineteenth and twentieth centuries' resistance against European colonialism. In recent years, the popular movie "Lion of the Desert," known in the Muslim world as *Umar Mukhtar*, and the controversial policies of leader Moamar Qadafi have contributed to strengthening the image of Libya as a land of resistance.

Moreover, the first casualties among the Glenville snipers who attracted national attention were black Muslims' readily identified names: Amir Ibn Katir and Malik Ali Bey.[20] Obviously, the Muslim influence, as seen in the Moorish Science Temple, the Nation of Islam and later Malcolm X's philosophy of resistance, was clearly apparent in subsequent black nationalist groups such as the Black Panther Party on national level and Ahmad Glenville riot in Cleveland.

In 1974, while observing the Muslim celebration of the holy month of Ramadan in Cleveland, the Cleveland Press reported, "Blacks originally adopted Islam to satisfy their need for cultural identity. But the Black Muslim movement today also embraces revolutionary social demands for blacks."[21]

Needless to say, the Nation of Islam was a driving force, but not the sole source of black conversion to the religion of Islam in Cleveland. Although Temple of Islam No. 18 at East, 106th Street and Superior Avenue was the center of black Muslim activism during the 1960's, it was the First Cleveland Mosque and its Moslem Ten Year Plan that led the transformation from black nationalism based Islam to more mainstream practices in Cleveland.

Temple No. 18. It was established in 1957 by Minister Theodore Hamzah. The Temple is now located at East 142 Street and Kinsman Avenue. Minister: Richard Muhammad.

[The Nation of Islam is a non-orthodox group. Mainstream Muslims do not see followers of the N.O.I as adherents to the proper teachings of Islam.]

The first Nation of Islam temple in Cleveland was started in 1957 by a group of adherents to the teachings of the Honorable Elijah Muhammad. Elijah Muhammad summoned Tariq Hamzah, also known as Theodore Hamzah, from Youngstown to be the new minister of the Cleveland temple, then called Temple of Islam No.18.[22] In August 1958, the temple sponsored a visit of Elijah Muhammad to Cleveland, where he gave a speech at Cory Methodist Church. His talk focused on the Nation of Islam's theology which promised that black Muslims would lead the salvation of the black race from the wilderness of North America. Elijah Muhammad dismissed integration with whites whom he called devils on earth. A local newspaper reported that "the atmosphere during this historical service was pregnant with contempt and hatred for the white audience."[23]

The local African American leadership protested strongly against using this historic church to host men that they considered "hate-preachers." *Call & Post,* a leading local black newspaper, received numerous letters and telephone calls protesting the visit. The newspaper invited the Reverend Howard Jones, a former pastor of the Smooth Memorial Christian Missionary Church, to share his eyewitness account of the event. Reverend Jones was "searched by the black Muslims from head to toe," the newspaper reported.

However, Reverend Jones gave a detailed account of the supreme leader of the Nation of Islam's visit to Cleveland. He expressed his mixed feelings toward the growing black Muslims, who preached hate and advocated the theory of black supremacy.[24]

The oral history in the area of Cleveland implies that Elijah Muhammad was not enthusiastic about making Cleveland one of the strongholds of the Nation of Islam. His earlier acquaintance with Wali Akram and the imam's nonracial orthodox teachings of Islam remained a factor in his reluctance to extend the Nation of Islam's influence in Cleveland.[25]

However, most followers of the Nation of Islam left the organization after Elijah Muhammad's death in 1975. They joined his son and successor Wallace Muhammad, an orthodox Muslim, who started reforming the beliefs and structure of the Nation, as well as its name.[26]

From the N.O.I. to *Sunni* Islam

By the time of the death of the supreme leader of the Nation of Islam, Elijah Muhammad, in 1975, the Nation of Islam was the largest Muslim organization in the United States. It had more than seventy-six temples nationwide with more than 100,000 members. However, this large and powerful organization quickly faced internal problems due to the adopted ideology dictated by the newly appointed leader Wallace Muhammad. Wallace Muhammad, a *Sunni* Muslim, envisaged transforming the Nation of Islam from black nationalist organization into a *Sunni* Muslim organization. In Cleveland, the new changes caused a rift in the organization and slowly fragmented the local branch of the Nation of Islam into four groups.

The first group was the majority. They comprised of those who accepted Wallace Muhammad's reforms. He changed the name of the Nation of Islam to the World Community of Islam in the West and led tens of thousands of African-Americans into a non-racial orthodox Islam.[27] In 1975, Minister Tariq Hamzah of Temple No.18 denounced Wallace Muhammad's orthodox vision of Islam and resigned from his position. Wallace Muhammad, who later became known as Imam Warith Deen Muhammad, summoned Malcolm X's brother, Omar X, from New York to replace Tariq Hamzah as Minister of Temple No.18. In 1977, Omar X resigned and moved to Detroit. Wallace Muhammad then called a minister from California known as Ali Rashid to lead his reforms in Temple No. 18, which by this time was known as Mosque No. 18. Ali Rashid was reluctant to transform the organization into orthodox Islam as dictated by Wallace Muhammad; he therefore resigned in 1979.

Minister Clayde X then replaced Ali Rashid at Mosque No. 18. Minister Clyde X, who is now known as Imam Clyde Rahman, succeeded in leading the transformation from black nationalist ideology to an orthodox Muslim community. In 1981, the organization completed the construction of Masjid Bilal on Euclid Avenue. This building was the first mosque to be built from the ground up. The project was made possible by community fund-raising efforts, donations by Masjid Bilal members, and land bought by former heavyweight-boxing champion Muhammad Ali.[28] This local branch of the largest African-American Muslim organization in the United States is still led by Imam Clyde Rahman.

In 1982, this community split due to administrative differences on how to implement the American Muslim Corporate Program (AMCOP) that Imam Wallace Muhammad mandated as an economic plan for the empowerment of the African-American community. In the mid 1980's some active members of the AMCOP agreed to form another mosque. This new community on Superior Avenue is called Masjid Warith Deen Muhammad. Imam Yusuf A. Ali is its spiritual leader.

The second group aligned itself with Louis Farrakhan and supported his call to restore Elijah Muhammad's pure teachings of Islam based on black nationalist rhetoric. In 1977, Farrakhan's revival movement started gaining followers among Clevelanders of the old Nation of Islam. In 1981, Roland Muhammad, a native of Darlington, South Carolina, who had joined the nation in the 1970's, became the appointed minister of Temple No. 18. This new Nation of Islam temple, however, currently does not play an influential role in the Cleveland Muslim community. Its homogeneous population is small compared with other orthodox communities. Nevertheless, the rhetoric of black nationalism remains vibrant in this community that targets poor, disenfranchised black youths of the inner city.

From left to right Imam Abbas Ahmad of the First Cleveland Mosque and Imam Yusuf Ali of Masjid Warith Deen Muhammad are shown celebrating the 65th commemoration of the First Cleveland Mosque and Imam W. Akram on July 19, 2002.

The third group sided with Tariq Hamzah, the first minister of the Nation of Islam in Cleveland, who broke away when Warith Deen took over the organization in 1975. Hamzah refused the transformation to orthodox Islam. He remained minister over his own temple that he established at the corner of Lee and Mayfield roads. He never joined Louis Farrakhan. Members of this group call themselves the true followers of Elijah Muhammad.

Finally, a large portion of the N.O.I.'s followers remained neutral and gradually turned toward the growing orthodox Muslims. Most of these people attend different mosques and do not consider themselves adherents of any particular Muslim community.

One of the leading communities in the transformation process from black nationalism to orthodox Islam was the Universal Islamic Brotherhood. This community was established in 1975 by Larry Thomas, better known as Diablo. Mr. Thomas was a controversial black nationalist leader who became Muslim in the late 1970's and joined the national organization of Dar-Al Islam led by Imam Jamil Al-Amin, formerly known as H. Rap Brown. Diablo, who became Imam Daud Abdul Malik, was president of the local Black Unity House. In 1983, Imam Daud, after acquiring property at Hayden Avenue in East Cleveland, invited area Muslims to join his Universal Islamic Brotherhood (UIB).

In the new location, the drug rehabilitation house was transformed into Masjid Al-Haqq or Masjid Haqq. A school was formed in 1985 under the name of the Islamic School of the Oasis (TISO) and Sheikh Masoud Laryea of Ghana became its spiritual leader. Next door to the school and mosque was a four-story apartment building that accommodated Muslim families who had joined the Universal Islamic Brotherhood community. In 1994, Imam Daud decided to make *hijrah*, migration, to Sudan and nominated Ali Omar from Nigeria to serve as acting imam of the community and principal of the Islamic school. The community adopted an inner-city Islamic *Shariah* that governs the life-style of its members. The UIB has focused on converting street gangsters, ex-convicts, and drug addicts.[30]

The organization also started an International Student Exchange Program. Between 1993, and 1995, it sent more than twenty students, Muslims and non-Muslims, overseas to study Arabic language, Islamic studies, and African history.

However, the community soon split due to a power struggle between Imam Daud, the founder and executive director who had returned form his hijrah, and most members of the community, who insisted on limiting his influence on the school administration. In May 1996, Imam Ali Omar was chosen by most members of the community as its new leader, and the new community left UIB and Masjid Al-Haqq and started a new Islamic school called Cleveland Community Islamic School (CCIS) which is currently located in the First Cleveland Mosque.

Notes

1. See William Dudley, *African American Opposition Viewpoints* (San Diego: Green Haven Press, 1997), pp. 228-239.

2. For more, read *Malcolm X: The Man and His Times.* Ed. John Henry Clark, (New York: Macmillan Publishing, 1969).

3. Claude Brown, *Manchild in the Promised Land* (New York: Touchstone, 1965), p. 336.

4. In 1963, Elijah Muhammad suspended Malcolm X from his position as national speaker and minister of the Nation. After 90 days of complete silence, Elijah Muhammad and his entourage extended the suspension to an indefinite period. This attitude from Muhammad was seen as encouraging Malcolm X to leave the Nation of Islam. In his first public appearance after his long silence, Malcolm X stated, "Internal differences between me and the Nation of Islam forced me out of it. I did not leave of my own free will." For more, see Karl Evanzz, *The Judas Factors: The Plot to Kill Malcolm X* (New York: Thunder Mouth Press, 1992), pp. 209-212.

5. Mattias Gardell, *In the Name of Elijah Muhammad: Lois Farrakhan and the Nation of Islam* (Durham, NC: Duke University Press, 1996), pp. 66-68.

6. For more details, see Kareem Abdul-Jabbar and Peter Knobler, *Giant–Steps: the Autobiography of Kareem Abdul-Jabbar* (New York: Bantam Books, 1983).

7. See Sulayman Nyang, "Islam in the United States of America: A Review of the Sources," *Islam in North America: A Sourcebook*, edited by Michael A. Koszegi and J. Gordon Melton (New York: Garland Publishing 1992), pp. 12-13.

8. Claude Brown, pp. 330-331.

9. For more details, read Imam Jamil Al-Amin, *Revolution by The Book* (Maryland: Writers' Inc., 1993), pp. x-xviii. Also read H. Rap Brown (Jamil Al-Amin), *Die Nigger Die!* (Chicago, IL, Lawrence Hill Books, 2002).

10. Eldridge Cleaver, *Soul On Ice* (New York: Dell Publishing, 1968), pp. 57- 66.

11. Robert Scheer, *Eldridge Cleaver: Post-Prison and Writings and Speeches* (New York: Random House, 1968), p. IX.

12. The alliance was called "Operation Black Unity" and the chair was Rabbi David Hill, a black preacher of Judaism.

13. Interview with Tariq Salim Ziyad on January 23, 1999. Ziyad, a long-time neighborhood activist, is the coordinator of "The Men Talk" group in Cleveland.

14. Martha Lee, *The Nation of Islam: An American Millenarian Movement* (Syracuse, NY: Syracuse University Press, 1996), p. 39.

15. Louis H. Masotti, and Jerome Corsi, *Shoot-out in Cleveland: Black Militants and the Police* (Washington: U.S Government Printing Office, 1969), p. 39.

16. Alex Haley, *The Autobiography of Malcolm X* (New York: Grove Press, 1993), p. 319.

17. *The Call & Post* (April 11, 1964).

18. See Malcolm X's speech in Cleveland titled the "Ballot or the Bullet," *The Call & Post* on April 11, 1964, published excerpts of the speech.

19. *The Plain Dealer* (April 4, 1964).

20. Louis H. Masotti, and Jerome Corsi, pp. 49, 51.

21. George Plagenz, "Allah Be Praised From Union Ave" *The Cleveland Press*, (October 19, 1974), p. 5.

22. *The Plain Dealer*, Sunday Magazine (August 21, 1994), p. 10.

23. *Cleveland Call & Post* (October 11, 1958), p. 6.

24. Ibid, p. 6.

25. Several figures in the Muslim community of Cleveland, including Imam Akram's older son Mahmud, are convinced of this aspect, even though I have not yet found any written documentation to support it. However, the reluctance of the leadership of the Nation of Islam to such a potentially important city as Cleveland tends to support this claim.

26. Allen Ernest, "Religious Heterodoxy and Nationalist Tradition: The Continuing Evolution of the Nation of Islam," *The Black Scholar* (Vol. 26, No. 3-4), p. 2.

27. Sonsyrea Tate, *Little X: Growing Up in the Nation of Islam* (New York: Harper Collins Publishers, 1997), p. 131.

28. Interview with Imam Yusuf Ali of Masjid Warith Deen, March 11, 1999.

29. *The Plain Dealer*, August 21, 1994, p. 10.

30. Interview with Imam Ali Omar, former principal of the Islamic School of the Oasis, March 13, 1999.

Chapter 5

Muslim Immigrants

Allah be Praised from Union Ave.
It was the Feast of Ramadan all over the Moslem
world – from the busy boulevards of Cairo to the dunes of
the Nafud desert of Saudi Arabia to Union Ave. in Cleveland.

[*The Cleveland Press*, October 19, 1974]

Reconciling Faith and Space

When discussing Muslim immigrants in the United States, the first picture that comes to mind is the Arab community. However, Arabs represent only a small portion of the estimated 1.3 billion Muslims worldwide. According to a 1989 study prepared by the Islamic Affairs Department of the Embassy of Saudi Arabia in Washington, DC, only eighteen percent of Muslims are in the Arab world; Turkey, Iran, and Afghanistan account for ten percent of the non-Arab Middle East; thirty percent live on the Indian subcontinent; twenty percent in sub-Saharan Africa; seventeen percent in Southeast Asia; and ten percent in China and countries of the former Soviet Union.[1]

The false perception that most Muslims are Arabs and all Arabs are Muslims has some historical basis. Because the Prophet of Islam was an Arab, and the Qur'an and most Islamic sciences are in Arabic which was the administrative language of the earlier Islamic states, Arabs are traditionally known as *izzul Islam*, meaning they were honored by Islam. The spread of Islam followed the movement and migration of the Arabs worldwide. Historically, their early migrations to Persia, Southeast Asia, North and East Africa and Al-Andalus (Spain) opened new chapters for Islam in these parts of the world.

The Muslim community in the United States is not predominantly Arab, and most Arabs in the United States are not Muslims. The U.S community reflects the complexity and diversity of Muslims worldwide. It is far from being monolithic. It is derived from *Sunni*, *Sufi*, and *Shi'i* sects and from diverse ethnic groups and cultural backgrounds. Although ninety percent of Arabs worldwide are Muslims, most of them in the United States are not. Some seventy-seven percent are Christian, according to a 2000 survey by the Arab American Institute. Immigrants from Pakistan, India, and other South Asian countries and African-Americans make up the majority of Muslims in the United States.[2] According to "The Mosque in America," a 2002 report commissioned by Muslim groups, thirty-three percent of those active in mosques are South Asian, and thirty percent are black. Arabs account for twenty-five percent, whereas European immigrants, Africans, U.S.-born whites, and others make up the rest.[3]

In Cleveland, there are three immigration trends that continue to enrich the Muslim experience. These are Muslims from Sub-Saharan Africa, Muslims from the Indian subcontinent and Muslims from the Arab world. Although these immigration trends generally share the orthodox teachings of Islam, they are not equal in their impact on the local Muslim community. The level of experience, dedication, and commitment to the three duties of a Muslim – *Dawa*, (to bring others to Islam); promoting good and warding off evil, and *Jihad* (strive for the sake of Allah) – varies by immigrants' individual, cultural, and regional backgrounds.

Generally, Muslims who migrate from secular and less conservative societies, such as Turkey, Eastern Europe, Malaysia, South Africa, and some West African countries tend to be less involved in local Muslim communities of the adopted country. Muslims from less secular, more culturally conservative societies, such as North African countries, Egypt, Palestine, Sudan, Somalia, the Arabian Peninsula, and the Indian subcontinent, tend to be active and constantly involved with local Muslim communities.[4]

There are other factors that determine how mosques are established among immigrant groups. Some of these are cultural, such as the growth of a particular group with a common ethnic or regional background, motivation and dedication to support an Islamic institution. Establishing a mosque or Islamic center also is a way for immigrants to adapt and adjust to their new environment. Mosques, traditionally, represent the core of social reform and the center of political advocacy in the Muslim world. A visitor to the Middle East or North Africa would notice that mosques provide the only outlet for political advocacy and social protest against opresive regimes.

Nonetheless, mosques in the United States provide a meeting place for members of the faith and a common ground for institutionalizing Islam socially and educationally. The first step after establishing a mosque is to find an imam, a leader knowledgeable in the Qur'an and familiar with *Fiqh* (understanding of Islamic Jurisprudence). The first generation of imams in the early Muslim immigrant mosques came mostly from Al-Azhar University of Egypt; others came from Turkey, Saudi Arabia and North Africa. In recent times, imams have been members of American communities who spent years of education in the Islamic world.

Responsibilities of an imam include leading the daily prayer, counseling families, and providing Islamic counseling on family, social and financial matters and arrangement of marriage, etc. Mosques and Islamic centers also hold weekend schools, weekly seminars, and even full-time Islamic schools to provide Islamic education for children, promote inter-faith activities and collect *zakat* and donations for the support of the poor and the needy.

Muslim Immigrants from Sub-Saharan Africa

Immigrants from Sub-Saharan Africa bring a taste of *Sufism* to the American Muslim community. In 1964, Malcolm X invited Sheikh Ahmed Hassoun of Sudan as a teacher of orthodox Islam to the newly established Muslim Mosque Inc., but the assassination of Malcolm X in February 1965 ended Sheikh Hassoun's spiritual leadership.⁵ Therefore, the presence of Muslim immigrants from Sub-Saharan Africa is largely a recent phenomenon of the 1980's. Generally speaking, the migration from Sub-Saharan Africa to the United States in modern history has been small compared with other regions of the world. The first wave of African immigrants after World War II came from eastern Nigeria during the Biafara War between 1967 and 1970. Most of these immigrants were Ibos from the southeast, who were targeted by advancing federal troops. The migration trend since the Biafara War has remained low and scattered among English-speaking countries, such as Ghana and Nigeria, and has included those escaping the Apartheid system in South Africa. All of these groups are predominantly Christian.

The 1980's signaled the first wave of economic immigrants from traditionally Muslim countries of West Africa: Gambia, Senegal, Mali, Guinea, northern Nigeria, and northern Ghana. The impact of these Muslims has been on an individual level, rather than on collective or institutionalized levels. Grand *Sufi* sheikhs of West Africa have been able, through visiting their disciple immigrants, to create *Zawiya* (literally, a corner, a specified place where a *Sufi* sheikh receives his brotherhood) of Sufist orders in major American cities. Sheikh Hassan Niass of Senegambia is nationally known for his efforts in building bridges with American Muslims. The grandsons of Sheikh Ahmadou Bamba of Senegal also visit the United States frequently as guest speakers and lecturers at Muslim organizations and associations.

In recent years, the *Murid* order of Senegal has become one of the driving forces behind American converts in New York City. The group launched Radio Murid International and created the House of Islam, a three-story Harlem building where the Murid sheikhs from Senegal travel frequently to spread their Islamic teachings. Due to the growing role of the Murid community in revitalizing the old neighborhood of Harlem, New York City recognized the legacy of the order and proclaimed July 28 as Sheikh Ahmadou Bamba Day.⁶

At the national level, two Africans are recognized as leaders in the American Muslim community: Dr. Sulayman Nyang, who is a professor of African studies at Howard University and a former ambassador of Gambia in Saudi Arabia, and Dr. Abdullah Idriss, the former president of the Islamic Society of North America. Nyang is a dynamic social scientist with remarkable contribution to research concerning American Muslim history and culture. Idris, who came from Sudan, served as Toronto's director of Islamic education. He is a renowned speaker and a board member in several Muslim organizations in North America.

In Cleveland, Muslim immigrants from Sub-Saharan Africa are a part of the general Muslim population. Some of them play fundamental roles in introducing the *Sufi* aspect of Islam. Imam Daud Abdul Malick of Masjid Al-Haqq was among the first imams in the country to visit the *Tijania Center* of Kaolack in Senegal and he invited the center's leader, Sheikh Hassan Cisse, to Cleveland for several visits and public talks. In 1995, Imam Daud also hired seven Muslim teachers from Sudan, Zambia, Senegal, Namibia, Kenya, Somalia, and Nigeria to work as full-time teachers in various subjects at his Islamic School of the Oasis. Two of these teachers were women from Kenya and Namibia.

In the 1990's Hussein Akram, grandson of Imam Wali Akram of the First Cleveland Mosque, created a *Muridiyah Zawiya*. The group of mostly Africans and African-Americans organized *Thikr*, or weekend classes at the First Cleveland Mosque. Omar Diouf, a Senegalese businessman, who owns the Ethnic Arts Store at Warrensville and Cedar Center, sponsors yearly visits of sheikhs, mainly grandsons of Sheikh Ahmadou Bamba, to the Muslim community and the *Murid Zawiya* of Cleveland.

Among the Sub-Saharan African Muslims in Cleveland, two figures are distinguished in their dedication to promoting peace and harmony and disseminating the teachings of Islam among the local Muslim community. Imam Ali Omar of Nigeria became leader of

Masjid Al-Haqq in 1993, when the acting Imam Daud A. Malick moved to settle in the Sudan. Imam Ali Omar also became principal of the Islamic School of the Oasis. In 1997, he resigned to become the new principal of Cleveland Community Islamic School.

Sheikh Masoud Laryea of Ghana is one of a handful of *Hafiz* (one who memorizes the holy Qur'an by heart) in the Greater Cleveland and is a remarkable scholar of Islamic sciences. He is a graduate of Ummul Qura University of Mecca. In 1985, he helped Imam Daud of Masjid Al-Haqq establish the first recognized Islamic School in Ohio, the Islamic School of the Oasis, where Sheikh Masoud was the spiritual leader. In 1986 and 1987, he led the two first unified *Eid* prayers in Cleveland history. All community mosques in Cleveland arranged for a single public *Eid al-Fitr* prayer at Gordon Park in 1986 and at Masjid Bilal in 1987 and unanimously selected Sheikh Masoud to lead the prayer. He is the former acting director of Cleveland Community Islamic School and is an appointed imam at-large.[7]

Muslim Immigrants from the Indian Subcontinent

Immigration to the United States from the Indian Subcontinent became prevalent only in the post-World War II years. There were two main barriers to earlier immigration: cultural barriers such as Hindu phobia of crossing "black water" and immigration laws in the United States that were targeted at the so-called "Hindu Invasion". Immigrants from the Indian subcontinent and Philippines were not granted the right to become naturalized citizens until the Luce-Cellar Bill of 1946. The immigration quota permitted the admission of 100 Indians per year.

The earlier immigrants from India were mostly from Punjab, which is predominantly Muslim. They were referred to as "Hindus" to distinguish them from Native Americans. Among the first immigrants were the missionaries of the Amadiyyah movement, who, in the 1920's, introduced Islam to mainstream American urbanites. Most of these missionaries did not stay in the country permanently; they either moved back to the Punjab region or relocated in Europe.

The most significant wave of immigration from the Indian subcontinent came after India's independence from Great Britain in 1947. The Immigration Act of 1952, also known as the McCarren-Walter Act, extended the national origin quotas and allowed entire subcontinent Indian families to move to the United States.

Unlike those from the Punjab region, these immigrants were highly skilled laborers and professionals and were religiously conservative. This new wave of immigrants was from Pakistan, India, and Bangladesh. According to Regula B. Qureshi and Saleem M. Qureshi, these groups were "characterized by dominant supra-local elite that had much in common across the regions, including primarily, religious ideology and practice."[8]

The attempts of these immigrants to create a social sphere for their religious ideology and elitism in their adopted country amounted to the significant institutionalization of Islam in North America. This group of immigrants was the initial driving force behind some of the oldest and most active Muslim organizations in North America today: Islamic Society of North America (ISNA) and Islamic Circle of North America (ICNA). ISNA, founded in 1982, today represents an umbrella of local and regional Muslim organizations in the United States and Canada. ICNA started as an Urdu speakers' organization in 1970's. By 1980, its constitution was changed from Urdu, which was the official language, to English, starting a new phase of extending the organization to other Muslim groups. The majority of the leadership in these organizations are descendants or immigrants from the Indian subcontinent. Furthermore, Muslims of this region represent the core of Muslim American professional organizations, such as the Islamic Medical Association, the Association of Muslim Social Scientists, and the Association of Muslim Scientists and Engineers.

In Cleveland, as elsewhere in the nation, Muslim immigrants have converged in single groups to establish mosques and communities. The establishment of the Islamic Center of Cleveland, Masjid Al-Islam, and the Muslim Association of Cleveland East (MACE) have provided good examples of the concerted effort among immigrants from the Arab world, and from the Indian subcontinent to unite. Ahmad Said Ansari and Hassan Ridha, both from India, are among the main families who founded the Islamic Center of Cleveland in 1967. Among the historically known leaders of the Islamic Center of Cleveland are Dr. Ijaz Ahmad and Masuod Khan. Both are from India.

Muslim Immigrants from the Arab World

There were three waves of Arab immigrants to the United States. The first group was Libano-Syrian, who moved to the United States at the turn of the century. They were mostly Christians who initiated opening "mom and pop" groceries, convenience stores, and gas stations. These groups eventually assimilated into mainstream American society. The second wave of Arab immigrants came in the post-World War II years, after the state of Israel was established in 1948. This group comprised of mostly educated Palestinian professionals. The third wave of Arab immigrants followed the 1965 Immigration Act; they came from Egypt, Syria, and Palestine. The majority of these immigrants were less educated, more conservative Muslims, who strongly pursued the establishment of Muslim communities in their newly adopted land. They have had difficulty with the melting-pot tradition of earlier immigrants.

In addition to these three waves, about 14,000 Palestinians arrived in the Greater Cleveland in the 1980's and 1990's. Most of them moved to Cleveland from Detroit, New York City; a few had come from Beit Haninah and Bethlehem in Palestine. This group was generally less educated and more conservative than the rest of the Arab immigrants. Currently, this particular Palestinian group makes up most of the Arab merchants who own nine out of each ten grocery stores in poor, inner-city neighborhoods of Cleveland.[9]

Historical evidence indicates that Muslim communities in the African-American neighborhoods of Cleveland are older than those started by immigrant Muslims. The presence of Muslims from the Middle East is a recent U.S. phenomenon and did not influence African-American conversion to Islam. Rather, these immigrants remained a source of Islamic idealism as black nationalist groups shifted to orthodox Islam. In fact, skepticism and disdain toward Arab Muslims were part of the Nation of Islam's culture.[10] In the post-Nation of Islam era, several unifying factors and elements have brought the two communities together.

Nevertheless, in the 1970's, which was the high point of Arab migration to the United States, cultural nostalgia grew sharply among the newcomers.[11] Cultural identity with the motherland was among the main motives for creating early immigrant Muslim communities. Consequently, this nostalgia brought a new sense of ethnicity to Muslim communities in the United States. Professor Sulayman Nyang notes that immigrants participated directly in promoting ethnicity and tribalism within the American Muslim community and that "this manifests itself as the number of Muslims from abroad increase and the process of self-identification and self differentiation begins to be felt."[12]

This factionalism had a wider effect, extending to established Muslim communities throughout the country. This factionalism manifests itself in two levels: tensions between Muslim immigrants and African-American Muslims, and tensions within Muslim immigrant from different countries and cultural backgrounds.[13] This cultural tribalism was not only a result of the socioeconomic reality in the United States; rather, to some extent, it arose from two other factors: the Muslim immigrants' cultural backgrounds and the black nationalism heritage of most African-American Muslims.

These two factors that should not necessitate any conflict, eventually created tensions within the Muslim communities. For instance, the African American experience with "black churches" and "white churches" is widely translated into "black mosques" and "Arab mosques" in some areas of the country. In a survey about the Arab community's relationship with African-American Muslims conducted by a national Arab organization, one question asked whether black Muslims presented any problem in the community? All answers were negative.[14]

In Cleveland, the influence of Muslim immigrants from the Arab world is very recent in comparison to the already existing African-American Muslim communities. Historical documents about Islam in Cleveland often assumed a linkage between Islam and earlier Arab migration to this country. This assumption is understandable because ninety percent of the Arab world population is Muslim. However, it does not take into account the fact that early Arab immigrants established no mosques or Muslim communities in the Cleveland area. Most of the early Arab immigrants were either Christians or Muslim isolationists. The Islamic literature at the turn of the century considered the West, in general, *Dar-Alkufr* (Infidel land). Therefore, most of the *ulama* (Muslim scholars) prohibited Muslims from settling in non-Muslim societies. In rare cases, they urged Muslim immigrants to be isolationists among their temporary hosts.

In the history of Islam in America, the presence of Muslims or immigrants from the Muslim world cannot be used as a defining line for the rise of the religion or the establishment of mosques. In fact, the presence of Muslims in the United States was evident at the founding of this nation, but there is no evidence to support that they established mosques and Muslim communities in this country. Amir Nashad Muhammad, an Islamic historian, mentions several cases of Muslim presence in antebellum America.[15]

The Encyclopedia of Cleveland History states that the first wave of Arab immigrants arrived in Cleveland in 1895 and included various Muslim groups from Greater Syria.[16] Nevertheless, when discussing the rise of Islam in Cleveland, the given date in this source is 1920: "Their number remained small and their gatherings were largely informal."¹⁷ This informality opposes the tradition of Islam that requires its followers to establish institutions for worshiping and learning wherever they stay. Furthermore, throughout the history of Islam, mosques remain the center and most important symbol of Muslim communities.

Hence, the earliest Muslim communities in Cleveland cannot be traced to the earliest Arab immigrants, whose original birthplaces were the only evidence of their religious affiliation.

Evidently, among the Arab immigrants in Cleveland, the Muslim group was the last to establish its religious house. Between 1906 and 1928, the Arab Christian groups consisted of the Byzantine Catholics, Maronite Catholics, Antiochian Orthodox, and Arab Orthodox who officially established five different churches throughout the city. Most of these groups were from the Levant area (Lebanon, Syria, and Palestine), with the bulk of immigrants coming from Lebanon, where the Christian population represents the highest proportion of Arab Christians in a single Arab country.

Furthermore, these immigrants were divided across national identities in Cleveland. The eruption of violence in the Middle East during the 1970s opened a new chapter of unity and political activism in the Arab community. In that decade, politically active groups, such as the Cleveland Council on Arab American Relations, which became the Greater Cleveland Association of Arab-Americans, and the Syrian American Club were established. These two groups were a driving force in creating national Arab organizations that focused on the Arab-Israeli conflict.¹⁸ However, the inception of mosques and Muslim communities in Cleveland started in the 1930's under the Ahmadiyyah movement despite the fact that the Arab community had already been in Cleveland for at least four decades.

Educational institutes of Cleveland also played a role in attracting Muslim students who influenced the establishment of immigrant communities. By the late 1970's the national Muslim Student Association (MSA) had a campus branch among the foreign students of Case Western Reserve University (CWRU). Foreign Muslim students from the Middle East, Indonesia, and Malaysia created this MSA chapter. Their main goals were to help Muslim students carry out Islamic programs. Activities of this early chapter were primarily limited to students on campus.

Uqbah Mosque Foundation

In the early 1980's, Abdussamih Moet, an Egyptian professor in the Department of Material and Molecular Engineering at CWRU became the center of Muslim student activities on campus. He used his academic position to help MSA organize its activities on campus. They used conference halls for *Jumu'ah* prayer and sponsored several Islamic educational programs. Before long, the MSA chapter was able to organize *Jumu'ah* prayers constantly in Spartan Hall of the University Student Center. In some cases, imams were invited from off campus to lead prayers and give *Jumu'ah* sermons.

In the mid-1980's the MSA members were young, dedicated Muslims who grew up within the revivalist literature of the Islamic movements that swept the Middle East, North Africa, and Southeast Asia. The Malaysian Islamic Study Group and Muslim Arab Youth Association were the most active members of MSA at CWRU. Students from the Middle East were generally former active members in Islamic organizations, ranging from the Islamic Brotherhood in Egypt to groups that later produced Algeria's Islamic Salvation Front (Front Islamique du Salut) and Tunisia's En-Nahda. It was in the hands of these students that the MSA shifted focus from campus-based activities to community-oriented activities.

Five students played a leading role in transforming the campus group into the MSA of the Greater Cleveland, including Muslim students from Cleveland State University and Cuyahoga Community College. Nurud-Deen became the president, and Ali Ben Marzuqa became the general secretary. Both of them were from Algeria.

Abdullahi al-Farisi from Kuwait, and Kamal Shawi and Abdul Hakeem Bahlul both from Algeria, were also active figures in the group.

In 1987 and 1988, the group, through fund-raising dinners and personal donations, were able to raise $32,000, which was used to buy a flower shop in the University Circle area. The building was purchased under the North American Islamic Trust (NAIT) of Islamic Society of North America.[19] This old building became the official location of MSA of Greater Cleveland. It became the melting pot of Muslim immigrant families in the University Circle area. Religious activities were extended to include family picnics, conferences, and weekly seminars on Friday evenings.

In early1990's, Ramiz Al Islamboli, who came from Lebanon, replaced Nurud-Deen and became imam of the MSA Mosque, which became known as Masjid Uqbah. During this time, the mosque was no longer a student organization except in name. The membership was extended to non-student adherents, mainly those Muslims who were already active participants in the group programs. Eventually, most of the founding members graduated; some returned home, while others considered Cleveland or other cities in the United States their new home.

This mosque also became a member of the Cleveland Council of Imams, which coordinates activities and programs of mosques in the Cleveland area. Uqbah Mosque provides chaplainry services to area hospitals, including the Cleveland Clinic, and University Hospitals. In 1995, among other constitutional changes, the mosque set up a new administrative structure consisting of a board of trustees, executive committee and general assembly. The name of the organization was changed to Uqbah Mosque Foundation. Imam Islamboli was re-elected as president, and he led successful efforts to raise money for a new building. The Zaid Foundation of the United Arab Emirates donated $200,000 for the building, and several successful fund-raising dinners organized around Cleveland enabled the new building of Uqbah Mosque Foundation to finally come to life in 1999. The mosque has become the centerpiece of diversity and harmony in the Muslim community of Cleveland.

A lot of Muslim immigrants in the inner city, as well as in the surrounding suburbs of Cleveland, attend religious services in this mosque. African-American Muslims in the urban area are also active participants in the religious and social services of the mosque. Dr. Abdul Kareem of Tunisia, a former member of the MSA at CWRU, served as president of the Mosque between 1998 and 2002. Imam Ramiz Islamboli was re-elected in 2002 as president of the mosque.

The photograph of June 2000 shows a congregation at Uqbah Mosque Foundation which has become the centerpiece of diversity and harmony in the Muslim community of Cleveland.

The Islamic Center of Cleveland

During the early 1970's, notable active Muslim immigrants in Cleveland were mostly students living either in the University Circle area or around Detroit Avenue. They attended Friday prayers at the First Cleveland Mosque, and Imam Akram was commonly claimed as their spiritual leader.[20] According to the *Encyclopedia of Cleveland History*, fifteen Arab families joined formally in 1967 to start the Islamic Center of Cleveland (ICC).[21] Among these families was the Hasan clan, which consisted of forty families who had migrated from Al-Bireh, a village in Rama-Allah, Palestine, to the Greater

Cleveland area.[22] These Hasan families constituted the nucleus of the center. The first imam of the Islamic Center, Nitham Hasan, was one of them. Hashim Hasan, Tallal Hasan, and Ibrahim Hasan are other family members who were key figures in the history of the Islamic Center of Cleveland. The impact of the Hasan clan on the Muslim and Arab community in Cleveland was remarkable with the Islamic Center of Cleveland being among the families' most important legacies.

The Islamic Center of Cleveland today is one of the largest mosques in Northeast Ohio and one of the hallmarks of Islamic architecture in North America.

Its history embodies the pain and struggle of reconciling faith and space. It depicts the tension of establishing religious world views in a diverse, yet secular society.

Historically, the idea of the Islamic Center started in 1966, when several immigrant Muslim families, mostly from Palestine, Southeast India, and North Africa, decided to establish a permanent place for their religious services. Prior to 1966, according to Muhammad Said Ansari, these families rotated congregation services from house to house. During major Islamic holidays and ceremonies, they rented places in downtown Cleveland, such as a YMCA facility, for *Jumu'ah* and *Eid* Prayers.[23]

In 1966, Ahmad Amrah from Palestine, a Hasan clan member, led Nazam Ansari from Palestine, Ahmad Said Ansari from India, Hasan Raza from Pakistan, Ahmed Fellague from Algeria, Hamdan Humaidan from Palestine, Loutfi Amrah from Palestine, Riaz Ansari from India, and Salim Dervic from Yugoslavia to purchase a new place at 9400 Detroit Avenue and inaugurate the Islamic Center of Cleveland.

This newly purchased building was roomy enough for the small congregation, but the group was unable to fully pay the $24,000 cost of the building. However, in 1978, when King Khalid of Saudi Arabia came to the Cleveland Clinic for medical treatment, acting

Imam Qadi Zamzami, together with a delegation of ICC officers, visited him to welcome him to Cleveland. The king inquired about the progress of Islam in the city. Imam Zamzami, who was a retired Egyptian judge, referred to the need for financial support to pay off the already purchased building that housed the mosque. King Khalid agreed to cover the remaining $8,000 and commended the group for not using riba (interest) to realize their noble goals.[24]

Muhammad Rasulullah Islamic Society on 9400 Detroit Avenue. This is the community house of the Shi'tes Community of Cleveland. The Islamic Center of Cleveland was located in this building between 1967 and 1992.

Hence, the Islamic Center is the first orthodox mosque in the area to be established by a non-African-American community. By 1986, attendance at the Islamic Center of Cleveland grew to more than 1,000 followers, most of them Muslim immigrants from the Middle East, North Africa and Southeast Asia. Some of the members were

In this June 1999 photograph, members are shown building the Community Center of ICC.. Fund-raising and volunteerism are the driving force behind community projects.

foreign students at Case Western Reserve University, Cleveland State University, and Cuyahoga Community College. During this time, the Islamic Center became another meeting place and cultural center for Muslim foreign students in the Cleveland area. Throughout this period, the mosque had no official imams. Nitham Hasan of Palestine, Imam Zamzami of Egypt, Sheikh Salih Nawwash of Palestine, and Sheikh Masoud Laryea of Ghana were among the best-known figures in the history of the mosque imamship. Other imams were foreign students who frequented the mosque. Abdussamih Moet of Egypt, Abdullahi al-Farisi of Kuwait, and Siraj Hussein of India were all CWRU students who were known as regular imams at the Islamic Center.

Masjid Al-Islam, an offshoot of the Islamic Center of Cleveland

Conflict arises very often in mosques that are established by Muslim immigrants due to two issues: doctrinal questions and leadership composition. However, mosques that are established by indigenous Muslims, usually African-Americans, do not often face these challenges because they are usually established by a single individual, one family, or a homogeneous group, such as ex-members of the Nation of Islam. In either case, doctrinal questions and leadership composition are already decided through right of ownership. In the Muslim immigrants case, heterogeneity of cultural backgrounds, level of religiosity and economic status are usually competing factors in the mosque administration.

Historically, the leadership of the Islamic Center of Cleveland has been composed mainly of professionals and merchants, who often prioritize the social mission at the expense of the religious mission. This tendency to have professionals preside over the administration of a religious institution generated conflict between old and new cultures, between homeland conservatism and the adopted-land realism.

In most countries of the Middle East, mosques are run by the *Wazaratul Awqaf* (the state department of religious affairs) which appoints imams as a method of keeping the mosque within state policy. The leaders of the mosque in the new land, also consciously or unconsciously, tend to duplicate the same administrative methods of the old world. That is, instead of delegating powers to mosque imams, the imams' roles are limited to religious matters. This, in fact, contradicts Islamic *Fiqh* which considers the role of the imam as the center in any decision-making process.

A major challenge that faced the administration of the Islamic Center of Cleveland in the 1980's was who had the upper hand in the decision-making process. Was it the executive committee – president, vice-president and members of the executive committee ? Or was it the imam, who gave the

Women praying at the Islamic Center of Cleveland (March 2002).

Sharia viewpoint on all matters? Or was it the general assembly, constituted from those who officially registered as active members of the community?²⁵ This conflict of views emerged in 1987 when the leadership decided to move the mosque to our new location at Parma, although most members of the general assembly objected to the new location and recommended sites closer to the downtown.

Eid Al-Fitr prayer inside Masjid Al-Islam (December 5, 2002). Maintaining straight lines and facing southeast toward Mecca are two of the main principles of congregational prayers.
(Photo courtesy: *Plain Dealer*)

In 1992, Sheikh Salih Nawash, one of the imams who were rotating leading prayers at the Islamic Center of Cleveland, and two executive members resigned from the administration of the mosque to start a new mosque, which they named Masjid Al-Islam.²⁸ In the same year, administration of the Islamic Center of Cleveland hired Imam

Fawaz Damra, a Palestinian and former imam of Masjid Taqwa in New York, to be the first officially appointed imam in the history of the mosque.

In 1995, at a cost of $2.7 million, the new Islamic Center of Cleveland opened in Parma to accommodate the spiritual needs of more than 5,000 Muslims. Imam Fawaz Damra has been an active spiritual leader and an interfaith proponent throughout his tenure at the Islamic Center of Cleveland.

The Muslim Association of Cleveland East

Imam Fawaz Damra, former imam of Masjid Taqwa in New York became the official imam of the Islamic Center of Cleveland in 1992.

The Muslim Association of Cleveland East (MACE) is one of the latest Muslim communities to be established in Greater Cleveland. In 1997, a group of Muslim professionals, mostly immigrants from the Middle East and the Indian subcontinent who lived in the eastern suburbs of Cleveland, envisaged establishing a mosque close to their work and home places.[27] The group led by Ahmad Banna, a cardiologist of Syrian origin and Anwar Rahman of Indian origin, started rotating their houses and offices as prayer places.

In 1998, they rented a room at a Ramada Inn in Mayfield Heights to serve as a temporary prayer place. The hotel room was used during *Jumu'ha*, *Maghrib* and *Ramadan-Trawih* prayers. In 2000, the group purchased its current building, which was formerly a lawyer's office to be used as the community mosque and established an Islamic weekend school.[28]

Notes

1. *Understanding Islam and the Muslims*, the Islamic Affairs Department of the Embassy of Saudi Arabia (Washington, DC: The Embassy of Saudi Arabia, 1989), p. 32.

2. See *The AMC Report*, published by The American Muslim Council Publication (Vol. 2. No. 2, 1992), p. 7.

3. For instance, see *Council on American-Islamic Relations Report 2002*, "The Mosque In America".

4. Iranian immigrants, generally speaking, represent an exception. The estimated 250,000 Iranians who opposed the Khomeini regime in 1979 and came to the United States around that time tend to shy away from Muslim communities. Many of them were students in the United States before the Islamic revolution in Iran.

5. See Louis A. DeCaro, Jr., *On the Side of My People: A Religious Life of Malcolm X* (New York: New York University Press, 1996), p. 233.

6. Sheikh Ahmadou Bamba is one of the most eminent Muslim reformists of the 19th century. He was born in 1853 in Senegal. His father was a well-known Muslim jurist who taught Islamic sciences, theology, mysticism, jurisprudence and *Nahwu* (Arabic grammar).

In 1883, Sheikh Bamba founded the *Muridiyah* sect, or the way of imitating the Prophet Muhammad (PBUH). The word Murid is derived from the word *irada*, which means, will in Arabic. It expresses the constant will to pull oneself from earthly possession to be totally devoted to Allah.

After the birth of *Muridiyah*, crowds started to flock around Bamba; therefore, he left the city of Mbacké, his birthplace, and founded the city of Touba in 1887 to accommodate his growing number of disciples. This increasing popularity brought the resentment of the French governor toward the sheikh who, according to a French report, undermined colonial authority and public order. The sheikh was accused of preparing his followers for *Jihad* against the French occupation. The sheikh was straightforward in his protest: "If you accuse me of waging a holy war, I declare you right. I do wage war to please Allah. But I do it by means of peace, spreading knowledge and reverential fear: the Lord by excellence is my witness." See his book *Masalikul-Jinan* (Senegal, Pikine: Mourid Press, 1987).

On September 5, 1895, the French Council of the Colony of West Africa decided to exile the sheikh to the rainforest of Gabon, in central Africa, as means of isolating him from his followers. On November 11, 1902, the sheikh was returned to Senegal because his presence in Gabon introduced Islam to this part of Sub-Saharan Africa. However, the sheikh was re-exiled to Mauritania on June 3, 1903. The French strategy was that Mauritanians were Muslim Arabs; therefore, the black sheikh would have limited influence in this hostile land. But this strategy backfired, according to oral history and writings of Mauritanians scholar Sheikh Sidiya Baba. The entire country of Mauritania rejoiced at the arrival of Sheikh Bamba. See Baba's account in *Diwanu-As-Sukhra* (Senegal, Pikine: Mourid Press, 1995).

On April 4, 1907, the sheikh was returned to Senegal and put under house arrest for the rest of his life. He passed away on July 19, 1927. One of the most amazing chapters in his life was that, although he spent more than three decades of his life in the hands of the French, he wrote extensively on societal models of Muslim communities. His legacy is profound in the modern life of the Senegambian region.

7. Throughout the book, several interviews were conducted with Sheikh Masoud Laryea concerning the history of Islamic education in Cleveland.

8. Regula B. Qureshi and Saleem M. Qureshi, "Pakistani Canadians: The Making of a Muslim Community," *The Muslim Community in North America*, edited by Earl. H. Waugh et all (Alberta, Canada: The University of Alberta Press, 1983), p 132.

9. Michael Selz, "Sam Quasem Tries to Ease Tensions Between Arab-American Grocers and the Blacks They Serve," *Plain Dealer* (January 3, 1999).

10. Barboza, *American Jihad: Islam After Malcolm X,* (New York: Doubleday, 1994), p. 214.

11. Michael Suleiman, "Arab American: A Community Profile," *Islam in North America: a Source Book*, Ed. Koszegi, Michael and Melton J. Gorden (New York: Grand Publishing, 1992), p. 51.

12. *The Muslims of America*, edited by Yvonne Yazbeck Haddad (New York: Oxford University Press, 1991), p. 238.

13. Farah Ternikar, "Tribalism in Muslim America," *Islam in America: Images and Challenges*, edited by Phylis Lan Lin (Indianapolis: University of Indianapolis, 1998), pp. 43-45.

14. Emily Kalled Lovell, "A Survey of Arab-Muslims in the United States and Canada," *Islam in North America: A Source Book,* Ibid, p. 72.

15. Review chapter 2 of *Muslim in America.*

16. *Encyclopedia of Cleveland History*, Ed. David D. Van Tassel and John J. Grabowski (Bloomington: Indiana University Press, 1987), p. 39.

17. Ibid, pp. 39, 558.

18. For more details, read Marry Haddad Macron, *Arab Americans and Their Communities of Cleveland* (Cleveland: Cleveland State University, 1978), pp. 221-238.

19. Using NAIT to purchase properties is a common practice among Muslim organizations in North America. It is a way to prevent individual claim on the property. It is also an endowment that functions to enforce the Islamic concept of *Waqf,* which is setting aside property or income for charitable purpose. This *Waqf* allows ISNA through its offspring NAIT to maintain influence over a quarter of mosques in North America.

20. According to some documents at the First Cleveland Mosque, Imam Wali Akram and his representatives conducted several marriages among Arab immigrants. Most of those Arabs were from Lebanon, Jordan, and Syria. Also, early Muslim Student Association meetings used to take place at the First Cleveland Mosque. Imam Muhammad Yunus of Masjid An-Nur remembers attending MSA conference at the First Cleveland Mosque upon his arrival from his homeland of India in 1973. E-mail interview on February 12, 2003.

21. *The Encyclopedia of Cleveland History*, Op cit, p. 558.

22. See *Hasan Family Reunion 2000: a genealogy on the Hasan family.* Limited publication for family members.

23. Ahmad Said Ansari, a native of India and longtime teacher with the Cleveland Public Schools, is the longest ranking executive member of the Islamic Center of Cleveland. He moved to Cleveland from Florida in 1965. Phone interview on March 3, 2002.

24. The story of the meeting with King Khalid was related to me by Nitham Hasan, who now lives in Florida, during a phone interview on October 10, 2002, and by Ahmad Fellague who was the acting president of ICC at the time. Fellague was interviewed on February 10 and March 4, 2003.

25. There are two types of memberships in all mosques: Active membership involves registering, paying dues, and attending meetings. Regular membership is guaranteed for every Muslim regardless of gender and race. It entitles them to join prayer services and attend lectures, seminars, and all religious activities.

26. Interview with Sheikh Salih Nawash on November 7, 2001.

27. Interview with Anwar Rahman on December 27, 2001.

28. Phone interview with Dr. Ahamad Bana on October 3, 2002.

Chapter 6

Surveying the Muslim Community of Cleveland

Gathering the Data

The statistical part of this study is based on responses received from a survey I conducted in conjunction with the Cleveland Community Islamic School (CCIS). The survey was distributed during December 2001 and February 2002. Various mosques, schools, Muslim Student Associations, and *Halal* food stores helped distribute the survey. Some friends and students also volunteered to distribute the survey.

The mosques that participated are those eleven orthodox communities that are the subjects of this study: the First Cleveland Mosque, Masjid Bilal, Masjid Warith Deen, Masjid Ummatullah, Masjid Al-Mu'min, Uqbah Mosque Foundation, Masjid An-Nur, Islamic Center of Cleveland, Masjid Al-Islam and Muslim Association of Cleveland East (MACE), and Masjid Al-Haqq. Among these mosques, some allowed us to directly distribute the survey to the congregation during Friday prayer, which is the most attended prayer during the week, while other mosques preferred to distribute the survey themselves during their weekend programs.

Cleveland Community Islamic School, Muslim Students Association(MSA) of Cleveland State University and *Halal* meat stores, such as Holy Land and *Halal* Products, friends and students allowed us to reach those Muslims who do not attend mosques or affiliate with Muslim communities. However, out of 500 surveys distributed, roughly 400 were returned, and 339 were adequate for evaluation.

The survey consisted of seventeen questions. Survey questions focused on three main areas of interest: (1) ethnic identity, gender and educational background; (2) religious background; and (3) religious affiliation.

With regard to ethnic identity, gender and educational background, the survey asked the following questions:

1. Do you identify yourself as someone who is

    1. African American

    2. Native (Indian American)

    3. Caucasian American

    4. Hispanic American

    5. Other. Please, specify:

2. Are you

    1. Female

    2. Male

3. How old are you now? _____ (years)

4. What is the last grade of school that you completed?

    1. Did not complete high school

    2. High School

    3. College degree

    4. Graduate degree

5. Were you born in the United States?

    1. Yes

    2. No

With regard to religious background, the survey asked:

6. What was the religion of your father at the time when you were born?

    1. Muslim

    2. Christian

    3. Jewish

    4. Other. Please, specify: _____

    5. Don't know

7. What was the religion of your mother at the time when you were born?

    1. Muslim

    2. Christian

    3. Jewish

    4. Other. Please, specify: _____

    5. Don't know

8. Did your parents raise you from birth as a follower of the Muslim faith?

    1. Yes (If Yes, please skip to Question 10)

    2. No

    3. Don't know

The next set of questions is about the time when you first declared that you are a Muslim.

9. During which of these time periods did you first formally declare that you are a follower of the Islamic faith?

    1. 1960–1969

    2. 1970–1979

    3. 1980–1989

    4. 1990–1999

    5. Other. Please, specify: _____

10. Which place, if any, do you associate with your first introduction to the teachings of Islam?

    1. In high school

    2. At university

    3. While in jail/prison

    4. Other. Please, be specific: _____

11. Who is the person who first introduced you to the teachings of Islam? Please, specify the person's relationship was to you at that time.

    1. A friend

    2. Teacher

    3. Co-worker

    4. Family member. Please, specify: _____

    5. Islamic religious leader

    6. Other. Please, specify: _____

The next two questions are about the reasons that motivated you to convert to Islam.

12. Please write down the ONE aspect of Islam that was most appealing to you at the time you formally accepted Islam?

13. At the time that you first accepted Islam, was there any particular Islamic public figure that influenced your decision to accept Islam?

1. Yes. Please, give name of person: _____
2. Don't know.

With regard to religious affiliation, the survey asked:

14. Are you a member of any Masjid?

    1. Yes. Please give the name of the masjid _____

    2. No

15. Which masjid do you most frequently attend?

    1. First Cleveland Mosque

    2. Masjid Bilal

    3. Masjid Warith Deen

4. Masjid Ummatullah
5. Masjid Al-Mu'min
6. Uqbah Mosque Foundation
7. Masjid An-Nur
8. Masjid Al-Haqq
9. Islamic Center of Cleveland
10. Masjid Al-Islam
11. Muslim Association of Cleveland East (MACE)
12. Other. Please, specify:_____
13. Not affiliated with any masjid.

16. How often do you attend religious services?
1. Every day
2. Once a week
3. More than once a week
4. Other. Please, specify: Number_____

17. Do you attend Friday services regularly?
1. Yes
2. No

The Sample

The survey only includes orthodox Muslims, who are the dominant majority in the United States and also in Cleveland. Therefore, *Shi'te*, *Ahmadiyyah* and *Nation of Islam* Muslims were excluded from the survey. Respondents by ethnic identity comprise 166 African-Americans, 4 Native Americans, 17 Caucasian Americans, 5 Hispanic Americans, and 145 "others". "Others" represented mainly Muslim immigrants from the Middle East, the Indian subcontinent and other immigrant minorities from Indonesia, Malaysia, Africa and Eastern Europe. A handful of those were of Asian American background.

Ethnic Identity, Gender and Educational Background

Ethnic Identity

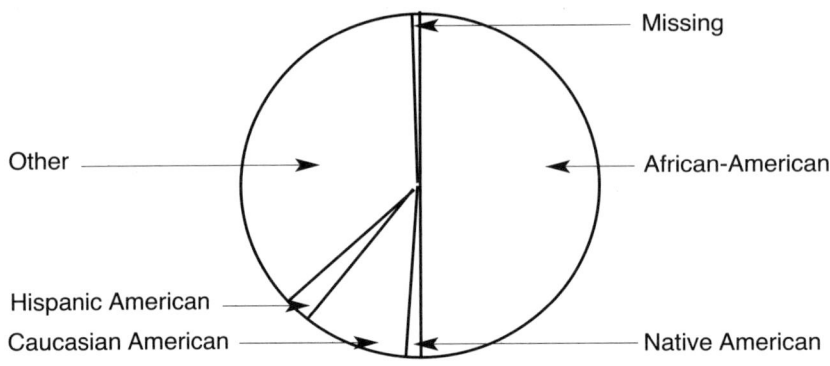

Ethnic Categories

The Muslim communities of Cleveland represent heterogeneous and multi-ethnic groups. Seven out of the 11 orthodox mosques are in the urban areas, where African-Americans are the predominant population; 49 percent of the respondents are African-Americans.

Ethnic identity	Number	Percentage
African American	166	49.0
Native American	4	1.2
Caucasian American	17	5.0
Hispanic American	5	1.5
Other	145	42.8
Missing	2	0.6
Total	339	100.0

Ethnic Categories of Respondents

One-third of the respondents were female while two-thirds were male. Ages ranged from 18 to 82. Sixty-three percent of the sample was born in the United States.

Age range	Frequency	Percent
18-29	102	30.1
30-39	108	31.9
40-49	50	14.7
50-59	41	12.1
60 & over	28	8.3
Missing	10	2.9
Total	339	100.0

Age Category

On the national level, African-American Muslims are about a third of the total Muslim population. Another factor that contributes to understanding those numbers is the demographic distribution of the population in Cleveland. According to 2000 census data, the total population of Cleveland is 478,403. That number is divided as follows: African-Americans are fifty-one percent, whites 41.5 percent, Hispanics or Latinos seven percent, American Indians and Alaska Natives are less than one percent, and Asians are one percent.[1]

According to the survey, conversion and immigration remain the main sources for the Muslim population in Cleveland. Close to two-thirds of the respondents are converts from either Christianity or Judaism, and over one-third of the respondents are Muslim immigrants. Eleven percent of the respondents are indigenous Americans who were born and raised Muslim.

Background	Number	Percentage
Muslim Immigrants	106	31.6
Muslims Born in the U.S.	36	10.7
Converts	193	57.6
Total	335	100.0

Source of the Muslim Population

On the national level, Muslim immigrants and their descendants are the largest constituent of the Muslim population, converts and U.S.-born Muslims are the second-largest constituent of Islam.

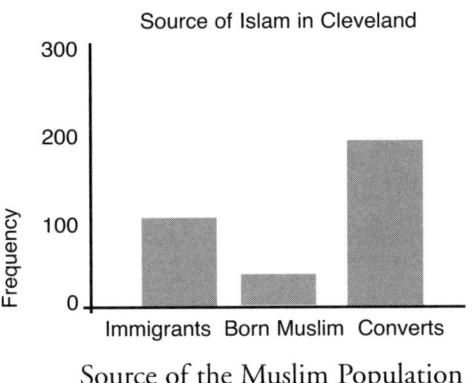

Source of the Muslim Population

Of the 145 respondents who claimed "other" ethnic backgrounds, thirty-two percent are Arab, twenty-six percent are Asian (people of the Indian subcontinent, Indonesia, Malaysian), twelve percent are Middle Eastern (Iranian, Turkish, and non-Arab residents), nine percent are African, two percent are European, four percent are unspecified, and fifteen percent identified themselves as Muslims, which reflects the Islamic notion that religious affiliation constitutes ethnic affiliation.

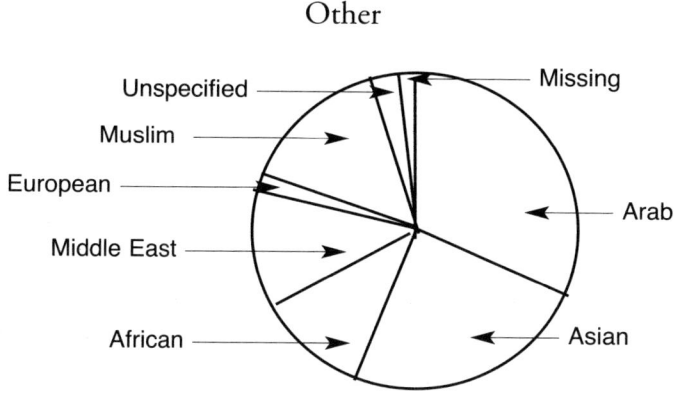

Others are those who do not claim American identity

Muslims in the United States include highly trained professionals dispersed throughout the private and public workforce. Likewise, in Cleveland, the sample indicates that Muslims are well-trained and highly educated: thirty-two percent of the respondents have a college degree, and twenty-four percent have a graduate degree.

Generally, the educational backgrounds of the Muslim community are not evenly divided across the ethnic identifications of those surveyed. Among Native Americans, twenty-five percent have a college degree and fifty percent have a graduate degree. Among African-Americans, thirty-four percent have a college degree, while nine percent have a graduate degree.[2] Among Whites, twenty-nine percent have a college degree and forty-seven percent have a graduate degree. Among Hispanics, sixty percent have a college degree, and twenty percent have a graduate degree.

Immigrants have a much higher educational level. Overall, thirty-two percent have a college degree, and thirty-seven percent have a graduate degree. Among Arabs, thirty-nine percent have a college degree, while thirty-seven percent have a graduate degree. Among Asians, twenty-three percent have a college degree, while fifty-seven percent have a graduate degree. Among Africans, forty-six percent have a college degree while thirty-one percent have a graduate degree. Among Middle Easterners, forty-four percent have a college degree, while twenty-eight percent have a graduate degree.

Religious Background

The sample reflects a high number of converts to Islam among African-Americans. However, there is a new generation, which has been raised in the religion of Islam in which the father or mother or both was Muslim. Of those U.S.-born raised in Islam, twenty-four percent are African-American, sixty-five percent are Caucasian American and seventy-five percent are Native American. Conversion/reversion to Islam remains the main reason for the growing number of Muslims among Americans.

Conversion/Reversion to Islam

Year	Frequency	Percent
1960-1969	24	12.4
1970-1979	54	28.0
1980-1989	29	15.0
1990-1999	64	33.2
2000	1	5
Other	21	10.9
Total	193	100

Formal Declaration of Islam

Among the American-born, twenty-seven percent of their fathers were Muslim, fifty-four percent of their fathers were Christians, and thirteen percent didn't know their father's religion. On the other hand, twenty-five percent of their mothers were Muslim while sixty-two percent were Christian.

Contrary to what most people think, the trend of conversion/reversion to Islam does not usually start in the mosque. Rather, converts usually come to the mosque to learn about Islam after accepting the *Shahada* at school, university, jail, or another setting. Among the converts, five percent associate their conversion/reversion to Islam with high school, ten percent with college, four percent while serving a jail term, and thirty-five percent mentioned other places.

Conversion/reversion also tends to happen within peer groups and among family members. Twenty-one percent of the converts say they were introduced to Islam by a friend, sixteen percent say a family member introduced them. Only six percent of the converts say an Islamic leader introduced them to Islam.

The nature of the Islamic message is also a factor in people's conversion/reversion. Twenty-one percent said Islamic teachings and the Qur'an were the most appealing aspect in their conversion/reversion, nine percent said the notion of submission to God, four percent said Muslim behaviors (i.e., they were influenced by the manner and behaviors of other Muslims), and three percent said the notion of *Salat* (prayer). Nearly twelve percent said other reasons.

The Nation of Islam also represents a transitional phase in some converts' journey toward orthodox Islam. As discussed in the previous chapter, the early generations of African-American Muslims were mostly from the Nation of Islam. Thirty-nine respondents mentioned Malcolm X, Elijah Muhammad, Louis Farrakhan, Muhammad Ali or Warith Deen Muhammad as public figures who influenced their decision to become Muslim. For instance, seventeen percent of those who converted between 1960 and 1969 mentioned Malcolm X, thirteen percent mentioned Elijah Muhammad, and seventeen percent mentioned others. Between 1970 and 1979, seventeen percent mentioned Malcolm X, nine percent mentioned Elijah Muhammad, six percent mentioned Imam Warith Deen Muhammad, and twenty percent mentioned others.

Religious Affiliation

It is important to note that for Muslims, attending a particular mosque is a matter of convenience and personal choice. There is conformity among the Ulama (scholars) of Islam that mosques are built for the sole purpose of worshiping Allah. Therefore, admission to a mosque is an equal right to all Muslims.

Membership in a mosque only implies volunteerism in making the place more convenient to the congregation. Therefore, some mosques have high membership while others have low membership. Generally, the more active a mosque is in organizing social, educational, or cultural activities, the higher its membership. The less active a mosque is in these matters, the lower its membership. Sixty percent of the respondents affirmed that they were active members, thirty-one percent said they were not, and nine percent did not respond.

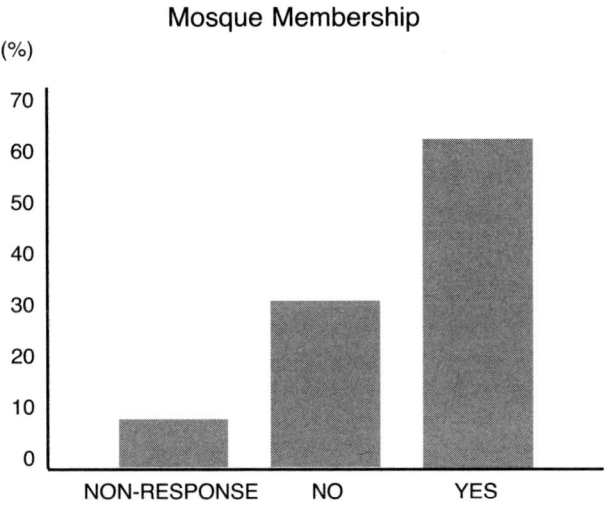

Survey respondents who consider themselves members in a mosque

In our sample, the leading mosques in terms of membership are also mosques with active educational, social or cultural programs. The Islamic Center of Cleveland had a weekend Islamic school with a registration of 425 students during the 2002 and 2003 academic year. Uqbah Mosque Foundation is a mosque with a full-time imam whose responsibilities include teaching Arabic and Islamic studies. Uqbah also organizes Friday evening lectures and seminars on a variety of issues. Masjid Al-Mu'min is active in fighting neighborhood gangs and teen delinquency. First Cleveland Mosque is one of the most liberal mosques in the area. It is active in educating women and strengthening family ties. The mosque also hosts a full-time Islamic school, the Cleveland Community Islamic School.

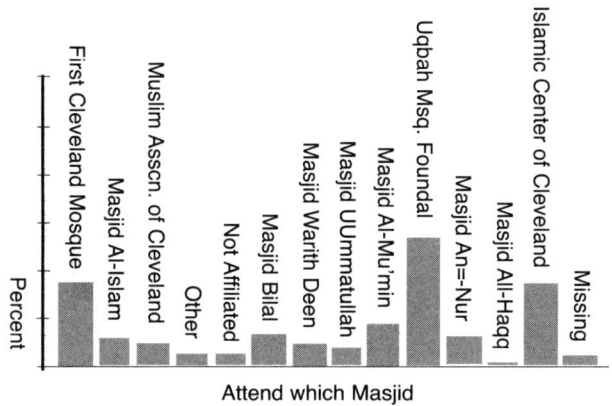

Attendance among the eleven
Cleveland-area mosques studied

The sample also shows a high level of religiosity in the Muslim community. A Qur'anic verse equates greater frequency of mosque attendance with greater faith.[3] Muslim social scientists usually use frequency of mosque attendance as a proxy for religiosity. Seventeen percent of respondents attend the mosque every day, twenty-five percent attend more than once a week, and forty-two percent attend once a week.

Frequency of Mosque Attendance

Frequency	Percentage
Every day	17.4
Once a week	41.9
More than once a week	25.1
Other	12.7
Missing	2.9
Total	100.0

Frequency of Mosque Attendance among Respondents

To have a better understanding of these numbers, let's compare them with other surveys on the same issue. A 1980's survey of Midwest and East Coast Muslims asked, "How often on the average did you attend a prayer service or Islamic class at any mosque/Islamic center during the past year?" Ten percent of the respondents said never, twenty percent said just on Eid, and thirty-nine percent said once a week.[4] In a similar survey, a decade later covering Muslims in Los Angeles, sixteen percent said several times a year, sixty-three percent said once a week or more, and eight percent said twice a month.[5]

Similar to that is the high attendance at Friday prayer, which is always called for during work hours. The earliest time that mosques in Cleveland start Friday service is at 12:30 p.m. and the latest time services start is at 1:30 p.m. Seventy-eight percent of the respondents said they attend Friday prayer while only twenty percent said they do not.

Levels of religiosity also vary from group to group. The most religious group in the survey, measured in terms of frequency of attendance, are African-Americans, followed by "others" (who are mostly Muslim immigrants), Caucasians and, last of all Hispanics and Native Americans. Among Muslim immigrant groups, the most religious are Arabs, followed by Asians and Africans.

On the whole, Cleveland mosques are not yet a melting-pot of the heterogeneous Muslim community. Although there is a growing diversity in the mosques, the Islamic multiracial idea has yet to be reached. Two factors explain the slow racial integration in Cleveland mosques. First, Cleveland is regarded as one of the most segregated cities in the United States.[6] This, in turn, affects integration of the racially and economically diverse Muslim communities. Second, historically, mosques were created by each ethnic group: African-Americans first and Muslim immigrants second.

The first comprehensive survey of U.S. Muslims conducted by Professor Ihsan Bagby indicates a national trend in convergence among these groups.[7] On a national level, there is an emerging ethnically diverse popular leadership. American Muslims are familiar with four leading advocates of Islamic issues. They are Dr. Jamal Badawi, an Egyptian Muslim; Imam Siraj Wahhaj, an African American Muslim; Imam Hamza Yusuf, a white American; and Dr. Abdalla Idris Ali, a Sudanese Muslim.

Nonetheless, our survey shows that Cleveland mosques are heading toward the multiracial ideal. Larger mosques are frequented by diverse ethnic groups. The most heterogeneous mosque in Cleveland is Uqbah Mosque Foundation, where thirty-eight percent of those attending services are African American, two and a half percent are Caucasian Americans, and fifty-eight percent are "others."

Mosques	African American	Native American	Caucasian American	Hispanic American	Other	Total
First Cleveland	68.4%	1.8%	3.5%	3.5%	22.8%	100%
Masjid Al-Islam	16.7%	----------	11.1%	----------	72.2%	100%
MACE	13.3%	----------	13.3%	----------	73.3%	100%
Masjid Bilal	81%	9.5%	----------	----------	9.5%	100%
Warith Deen	85.7%	----------	----------	----------	14.3%	100%
Masjid Ummatullah	90%	----------	----------	----------	10%	100%
Masjid Al-Mu'min	92.6%	3.7%	----------	----------	3.7%	100%
Uqbah Mosque	38%	----------	2.5%	----------	58.2%	99%
Masjid An-Nur	88.9%	----------	----------	----------	11.1%	100%
Masjid Al-Haqq	100%	----------	----------	----------	----------	100%
Islamic Center	3.6%		14.3	1.8	80.4%	100%
Other	62.5%	----------	----------	12.5%	12.5%	100%
Not affiliated	50%	----------	----------	12.5	37.5	100%

Cleveland area Mosques' attendees distributed across Ethnic Groups

Cleveland Muslims come from an array of ethnic, cultural and national backgrounds, mosques should strive to present that complex picture in their congregations. Programs such as weekend schools, evening lectures and open house discussions have proven to be vital components for creating a diverse community mosque.

Notes

1. July 2000 U.S. Census.

2. The high number of graduates among Native American is due to the small number of native participants in the survey.

3. Qur'an, 9:18.

4. Yvonne Yazbeck Haddad and Adair Lummis, *Islamic Values in the United States: A Comparative Study* (New York: Oxford University Press, 1987), p. 27.

5. Kambiz Ghanea Bassiri, *Competing Visions of Islam in the United States: A Study of Los Angeles* (Westport: Greenwood Press, 1997), p. 64.

6. In 1990, the *Black Isolation Index* ranked Cleveland as the second-most segregated city in United States. A *Detroit News* analysis of 2000 Census data also ranked Cleveland as the fifth, most segregated city in the nation.

7. See "The Mosque in America: A National Portrait," published by the *Council for American Islamic Relations,* 2002, available at http://www.cair-net.org/mosquereport.

Conclusion

Challenges and Prospective

The history of Islam in Cleveland is similar to that of Islam in other major American cities, such as New York, Chicago, and Detroit. It is a cumulative experience of inner-city inhabitants searching for socio-cultural alternatives, and Muslim immigrants trying to reconcile their Islamic faith with North America's secular space.

The rapid growth of the Muslim faith in the United States stems in part from the similarity between America's inner cities, where most conversions take place, and third-world major cities, where most Muslim immigrants come from. This similarity reduces the cultural and economic gap between inner-city residents and Muslim immigrants, thus paving the way for interaction, acculturation, and conversion. Although most black conversions/reversions to Islam start in urban places, most white conversions/reversions to Islam occur on university campuses and in academic settings. The former represents more than two-thirds of America's converts to Islam while the later represents a tiny number of the converts.

In Cleveland, the growth of the Muslim faith is evident in how one community mosque with a handful of followers at the second decade of the twentieth century mushroomed by the turn of the twenty-first century into eleven orthodox community mosques and two non-orthodox community mosques with an estimated 50,000 followers. The same factors that explain this growth also explain the national growth of the Muslim community during the same period from a few hundred to several million followers.

Although Islam remains the fastest-growing religion in America, it is still portrayed in the mass media as the religion of "others." Obviously, otherness is the most fertile soil in which to breed prejudice, discrimination, and intolerance. This labeling creates the challenge of establishing a community of believers who are proud of their national identity as Americans and comfortable in their religious affiliation as Muslims. As Imam Jamil Al-Amin, formerly known as H. Rap Brown, former chairman of the Student Nonviolence Coordinating Committee (SNCC), puts it, "No longer can America only acknowledge Judaism and Christianity as its only major faiths. Islam must also be included and recognized for its worth. America must respect its own diversity. Our nation's inclusion and future in the world community may count on it."[1]

Centuries-old prejudices are rampant in the mass media's propaganda that makes the mainstream society skeptical of Islam. This is the conventional norm in the Western media which focus on the basic distinctions between "West" and "East" as the media, either intentionally or inadvertently, promotes the belief that Islamic values are threatening to the very existence of America's Judeo-Christian heritage. But Islam is a faith, not a territory. Furthermore, Islam does not require geographical and racial labels or boundaries. Therefore, to treat Islam as an Arab or Middle Eastern religion makes sense only in a historical sense.

In theory, Islam is introduced in the Qur'an as the "religion of all humanity." In practice, more than two-thirds of the Muslim world's population lives in areas other than the Middle East and North Africa. As British scholar Karen Armstrong, notes:

> It is natural to explain another culture in terms of one's own but these ludicrous remarks are not so dissimilar in spirit from popular distortions of Islam that are current in our own day, which tell us rather more about our own Western preoccupation, prejudices and anxieties than they tell us about Islam stigmatized for being an excessively and essentially violent religion or for being inherently opposed to rationality and progress.[2]

Frankly, Islam is not an antithesis to America as the ill-informed media suggest. Likewise, America is not an infidel land, as some groups would have it. What in the following teachings of Islam would offend any American?:

> There is no compulsion in matters of religion.[3] Bear witness to the truth in all equity and never let hatred of others lead you to deviate from Justice. Be just for this is closest to righteousness. Remember God is well aware of all that you do.[4]

> Oh, Mankind! We created you from a single soul, male and female, and made you into nations and tribes, so that you may come to know one another [not to despise each other]. Truly, the most honored of you in God's sight is the one who is most righteous.[5]

Further, in the last sermon of the Prophet of Islam in 632 CE, he made it clear that:

> All human kind is from Adam and Eve. An Arab has no superiority over a non-Arab, and a non-Arab has no superiority over an Arab. A white person has no superiority over a black person, and a black person has no superiority over a white person, except by piety and righteous actions.[6]

Similarly, what is anti-Islamic about the Declaration of Independence?

> We hold these truths to be self-evident, that all men are created equal, that they are endowed by their Creator with certain unalienable Rights, that among these are Life, Liberty and the pursuit of Happiness.

Moreover, who among Muslims would not embrace the Preamble to the American Constitution?

> We the people of the United States, in order to form a more perfect Union, establish justice, secure domestic tranquility, provide for the common defense, promote the general welfare, and secure the blessings of liberty to ourselves and our posterity, do ordain and establish this constitution for the United States of America.[7]

Obviously, there is nothing in those statements that a just Muslim country would not like to provide for its people.

The common ground between America's values and Islamic teachings lies in issues such as equality, mercy, and moderation. The mission of America, Dwight Waldo, the father of political theory of public administration, observes, "whether stated in religious terms or not, has been conceived as witnessing democracy before mankind, bearing democracy's ideals of freedom and equality, and its material blessing, to the nations of the world."[8] This mission does not contradict that of the Muslims, who, according to the Qur'an, are supposed to be "witnesses over humanity "[9] in disseminating love, mercy, and justice. Extremism is as dangerous to social order and world peace as it is to Islam itself. The message of Islam is meant to be "mercy for all mankind." And, according to the most classical explanations of the Qur'an, Muslims ought to be "*Ummatan Wasata*" [10] – a moderate nation, a nation in the middle – far from all sorts of extremism. Thus, moderation is one of the most significant virtues in Islam.

One can argue that this is a selective reading of Islam and that there are aspects of Islam that differ or contradict America's liberal values. I would agree to some extent, but differences do not necessitate clash.[11] Most of the so-called "clash of civilizations" between America and Islam or the West and the East, as Professor Bernard Lewis holds, are products of subjective interpretation by some to suit their own prejudices. This is similar to the way that the framers of the American Declaration of Independence interpreted the statement "all men are created equal" to exclude blacks and women.[12] Such a biased interpretation of any script only reflects human prejudice and immaturity, rather than the reality of the historical text. Equally, a Muslim leader who interprets the Holy Qur'an to make it anti-American is also expressing his inner prejudice rather than the spirit of Qur'anic teachings.

However, Muslims in America should not focus on the depiction or exhibition of Islam, but rather on the creation and application of Islamic values such as love, justice, and equality. Muhammad Abduh (1844-1905), an Egyptian scholar and founder of the Salafi movement, "The Nahdah Moveme", once explained to a group of journalists who confronted him on his return from a tour in the West, "I found Islam [in the West], but not Muslims, and in the Muslim World I found Muslims, but not Islam." Sheikh Abduh's remark still applies. Muslim Americans should lead the way in teaching the rest of the Muslim world lessons in freedom, political transparency, and rule of law. By the same token, Americans also should know that fundamentalism, oppression of freedom, and totalitarian rules in the Muslim world are the result of centuries, of backward thinking, cultural lethargy, and colonialism, and have nothing to do with the religion of Islam and its teachings. Unfortunately, in most Muslim countries, governments are monarchies, military dictatorships, or one-party systems. In general, many Muslims are safer and freer to practice Islam in America than they are in most Muslim countries.

To get a clear picture of the local community, I asked some active Muslims in Cleveland what were the challenges their communities faced. Although these individuals have different experiences and diverse cultural backgrounds, I found a thread of agreement among them: the community lack of unity in establishing educational and social institutions.

Imam Mutawaf Abdus Shaheed, who is the longest serving Imam in Cleveland and leader of Masjid Al-Mu'min stated, "Maintaining Muslim identity and becoming educated in the importance of segments of our society is a challenge." He also noted, "Being able to become self-sustaining and rejecting extremism will stabilize the Muslim community."

Imam Ramiz Islamboli, who came to Cleveland from Lebanon in 1985 and is currently president of Uqbah Mosque Foundation, cited several challenges facing the Muslim community of Cleveland. Imam Islamboli, who is also a Muslim chaplain in federal prisons, succinctly listed four challenges: "(1) absence of a common set of goals, (2) lack of representation in many branches of city, government offices and other social work, (3) lack of financial resources, and (4) lack of educational institutions and media outlets."

Hana Halabi, who came to the United States from Syria in 1974, and moved to Cleveland in 1980, is an active advocate of Islamic education in Cleveland. She is the principal of the Islamic School at the Islamic Center of Cleveland. In her view, Islam speaks for itself: "the basic teachings of the Qur'an and the Prophet Muhammad (pbuh) are the best way to present Islam." The biggest challenge that faces Muslims in Cleveland, she states, is "ignorance of Islam among most Americans including some Muslims. The attack on Islam by some groups mainly after 9/11 makes our job difficult. But we have to be somewhat optimist since more people are interested to know about Islam."

Sheikh Masoud Laryea, a native of Ghana, came to Cleveland in 1985 after graduating from Ummul Qura University of Mecca. He is among the handful of *Hafiz* (ones who memorizes the entire holy Qur'an) in Greater Cleveland. In his view, "The Muslim community of Cleveland faces the challenges of establishing educational, economic, and social institutions. These challenges, which usually require a concerted effort, are increasingly compounded by the prevalence of disunity in the ranks of the Muslim population of the city."

For Hajja Nurah Akram Abdulwahab, who is organizer of Cleveland Haj Group and the daughter of the First Cleveland Mosque founder Imam Wali Akram, the challenges of the Muslim community in Cleveland are clear and identifiable: "Many people need to understand that Islam is not a new religion, it is not a terrorist religion, but one found on peace and tranquility. Islam gives one the authority to judge between right and wrong."

Imam Muhammed Younus Ali of Masjid An-Nur, who came to Cleveland from India in 1973, describes the problem in national context: "The challenges that face the Muslims in Cleveland are the same in each city across America." These are, "(1) lack of concern for each other, meaning racial and cultural differences are allowed to separate; (2) difficulty in maintaining the belief in Islam in this environment; and (3) need to educate children in the Islamic way."

An analytical approach to the progress of Islam and the Muslim community in Cleveland traces these challenges to two roots. One is historical: the ways and methods by which Islam reached indigenous American Muslims, especially, members of the African American community. The other is political: Muslim immigrants' political activism concerning U.S. foreign policy, which indirectly contributes to galvanizing the domestic Muslim agenda.

In regard to the first, African-American involvement with Islam started in the era of black nationalist movements, whether in the Moorish Science Temple or in the Nation of Islam. In these groups, Islam has been seen as a racial component of being African and black in opposition to being American and white. Although times have changed, most of these generations have become *Sunni* Muslim, and the legacy of pure black nationalism died out in the 1970's. The effects of these groups have evolved into a self consciousness that continues to taint their approaches to Islam. In particular, most inner city mosques embody separatist tendencies.

In regard to the second, the political root is that Muslim immigrants and their descendants, who constitute the largest number of Muslims in this country, face the dilemma of dual emotions: love for the opportunity and freedom their country provides to its inhabitants, but disapproves the foreign policy their country practices overseas. In this love-hate relationship, Islam becomes the platform for political action. Ironically, this is not dissimilar to the old black nationalist strategy of using Islam as spiritual guidance.

This attitude has effects on national and community levels. On the national level, it alienates Islam from the mainstream public, which perceives it as a threat to unity and public interest. On the community level, it fragments unity of purpose among local Muslim leaders and creates a mushrooming of associations, communities, and political factions without any central leadership.

In Cleveland, mosques established by African-Americans have spearheaded action in fighting teen pregnancy, domestic violence, drug use, and other problems that plagued the African-American community. These issues are the daily challenges of all social and religious institutions in black neighborhoods, including mosques. International politics and organic affiliations with Muslim issues outside the United States are a secondary priority. On the other hand, because Muslim immigrants tend to live in affluent suburbs, they do not perceive the daily challenges that confront inner-city mosques to be relevant in their lives. But the backlash of homeland problems in Palestine, Kashmir, Bosnia, and Kurdistan, and Somalia are relevant to these American Muslims and are their main concerns.

Al-Mansur Abdurrahim, a second-generation African-American Muslim, explained, "Muslim immigrants think in terms of how does it affect my homeland and family that is still there, and the indigenous Muslims think in terms of how it is affecting them locally, right now, and today. Both views have merit, but in terms of Islam there should be only one view and that is Islamic brotherhood."[13]

Most notably, the Muslim community of Cleveland disagrees on the relative importance of foreign policy in the Middle East and on the Indian sub-continent as opposed to domestic issues, such as the crises of Cleveland Public schools, teen pregnancy, and the decline of the inner-city neighborhoods. A divergence of opinion clearly distinguishes suburban mosques from inner city mosques. While suburban mosques focus on high-profile political issues, and interfaith dialogues, neighborhood issues engage inner-city mosques.

However, Cleveland Muslims, like other American Muslims, must reach a consensus on their priorities. They should "think globally and act locally. That is the legacy of Malcolm X, and everyone should learn from it," to quote Khalid Abdul Samad's words, a community activist and organizer of Cleveland Peace in the Hood.[14] A racially and economically divided community results in political different agendas. Challenges identified by inner-city mosques, such as Masjid Bilal, Masjid An-Nur, Masjid Ummatullah, Masjid Warith Deen, Masjid Al-Mu'min, Masjid Al-Haqq and First Cleveland Mosque are fundamentally different from those in the outskirts of the inner city. However, these differences do not negate the fact that Cleveland Muslims, like Muslims elsewhere in this country, have a common denominator in being conservative in private issues and liberal in public issues. They can easily agree on a local agenda concerning stereotypes of Islam, discrimination, representation, and for protecting their rights as citizens of this country. Addressing these critical issues will secure them a recognized space in America's consciousness.

Notes

1. Russell Reza-'khaliq Gonzaga, " One Nation Under Allah," ColorLines (Vol 5. No. 3. Oakland: ARC Publications, 2002), p. 6.

2. K. Armstrong, *Holy War: The Crusades and Their Impact on Today's World* (New York: Doubleday, 1991), p. 470.

3. Qur'an, 2:256.

4. Qur'an, 5:8.

5. Qur'an, 49:13.

6. All versions of the sermon are available in several traditional sources as *Al-Bukhari* and *Al-Muslim*. Also read Muhammad Al-khudari's book, *Nuru-alyaqin* (Beirut: Darul-Jabal, 1987), p. 305

7. See Muqtedar Khan in a similar discussion, "Why Muslims Should Participate in American Government," *Iviews* (June 27, 2000).

8. Dwight Waldo, *The Administrative State* (New York: Holms & Meier Publishers, 1984), p. 15.

9. Qur'an, 2:143.

10. Qur'an, 2:143.

11. Most controversies about Islam promoting violence and killing people of other faiths come from misinterpretations of the Qur'an. People should understand that in the authentic tradition of Islam there are two sciences that need to be incorporated in reading the Qur'an: First, *Al-nasekh wal*

Mansoukh (the science of abrogation) enables a reader to understand that some verses in the Holy Qur'an have been invalidated and abrogated by other verses. Second, *Sababu an-Nuzul* (occasion of Revelation) helps a reader determine the period in which each verse or chapter of the Qur'an was revealed, thus understanding the circumstances for its revelation. These two sciences are fundamental in understanding the historical circumstances of the life of the Prophet of Islam. They capture the four periods of his life. The attribute of each period is evident from the verses revealed in that period, whether in war or peace.

12. On this point, read Roger Wilkins, *Jefferson's Pillow: The Founding Fathers and the Dilemma of Black Patriotism* (Boston: Beacon Press, 2001), pp. 9–33.

13. E-mail interview on March 13, 2003.

14. In a public comment after 2001 *Eid al-Fitr* prayer at First Cleveland Mosque.

Selected Bibliography

Abdul-Jabbar, Kareem and Knobler, Peter; *Giant–Steps: the Autobiography of Kareem Abdul-Jabbar*, New York: Bantam Books, 1983.

Adib, Rashid; *Islam, Black Nationalism, and Slavery: A Detailed History*, Maryland: Black Muslim History, 1995.

Ajayi, J.F. Ade and Crowder, Michael; *History of West Africa.* New York: Columbia University Press, 1972.

Al-Amin, Jamil; *Revolution by The Book,* Maryland: Writers' Inc., 1993.

Alford, Terry; *Prince Among Slaves.* New York: Oxford University Press, 1977.

Ali, Amir Nashid; *Muslims In America: Seven Centuries of History*, Maryland: Amana Publication, 1998.

Alluri, Adam Abdullah; *Al--Islam Alyawma wa Qadan Fi-Nigerian* (Islam Today and Tomorrow in Nigeria), Cairo: Whaba Library, 1985.

Al-Sa'di; *Tarikh al-sudan Dawn* to 1613;translated by John Hunwick under *Timbuktu & the Songhay Empire*, Boston: Brill, 1999.

Armstrong, Karen; *Holy War: The Crusades and Their Impact on Today's World*, New York: Doubleday, 1991.

Asante, *Molefi Kete; The Afrocentric Ideas*, Philadelphia: Temple University Press, 1987.

Austin, Allan; *African Muslims in Antebellum America*, New York: Gardland Publishing, 1984.

Baldwin, James; *Notes of a Native Son*, Boston: Beacon Press, 1955.

Baldwin, James; *The Fire Next Time*, New York: The Dial Press, 1963.

Barboza, Steven; *American Jihad: Islam After Malcolm X*, New York: Doubleday, 1994.

Bassiri, Kambiz Ghanea; *Competing Visions of Islam in the United States: A Study of Los Angeles*, Westport: Greenwood Press, 1997.

Blyden, Edward W; *Christianity, Islam and the Negro Race*, Baltimore: Black Classic Press, 1994.

Boahen, A. Adu; *African Perspectives on Colonialism*, Baltimore: The John Hopkins University Press, 1989.

Brown, Claude; *Manchild in the Promised Land*, New York: Touchstone, 1965.

Brown, H. Rap (Jamil Al-Amin); *Die Nigger Die!* Chicago, IL: Lawrence Hill Books, 2002.

Clarke, John Henry; *Malcolm X: The Man and His Times*, New York: Macmillan Publishing, 1969.

Clarke, John Henrik; *Africans at the Cross Roads: Notes for an African World Revolution*, New Jersey: African World Press Inc., 1991.

Cleaver, Eldridge; *Soul On Ice*. New York: Dell Publishing, 1968.

Dannin, Robert; *Black Pilgrimage to Islam*, New York: Oxford University Press, 2002.

DeCaro, Jr A; *On the Side of My People: A Religious Life of Malcolm X*, New York: New York University Press, 1996.

Diouf, Sylviane; *Servants of Allah: African Muslims Enslaved in the Americas*, New York: New York University Press, 1998.

Dirks, Jerald, F.; *The Cross & The Crescent* : *An interfaith Dialogue between Christianity and Islam*, Maryland, Amana Publications, 2001.

Dirks, Jerald, F.; *Understanding Islam*: A *guide for the Judaeo-Christian Reader*, Maryland, Amana Publications, 2003.

Du Bois, W.E.B.; *Africa: Its Geography, People and Products and Africa: Its Place in Modern History*, New York: KTO Press, 1977.

Dudley, William; *African American Opposition Viewpoints*. San Diego: Green Haven Press, 1997.

Emerick, Yahiya; *What Islam Is All About*, New York: International Book and Tapes Supply, 1997.

Ernest, Allen; "Religious Heterodoxy and Nationalist Tradition: The Continuing Evolution of the Nation of Islam," *The Black Scholar* (Vol. 26, No. 3-4).

Essien-Udom, E.U.; *Black Nationalism: A Search for an Identity in America*, Chicago: The University of Chicago Press, 1962.

Evanzz, Karl; *The Judas Factor: The Plot to Kill Malcolm X*, New York: Thunder's Mouth Press, 1992.

Ferris, Marc; "Immigrant Muslims in New York City," *Muslim Communities in North America*, edited by Yvonne Yazbeck Haddad and Janet Idleman Smith, Albany: Suny Press, 1994.

Findley, Paul; *Silent No More : Confronting America's False Images of Islam*, Maryland: Amana Publication, 2001.

Fisher, Allan and Humphery; *Slavery and Muslim Society in Africa*, New York: Doubleday, 1971.

Friedmann, Yohanan; *Prophecy Continuous*, California: The University of California Press, 1989.

Fry, George and R. King, James; *Islam: A Survey of the Muslim Faith*, Michigan: Baker Book House, 1980.

Gardell, Mattias; *In the Name of Elijah Muhammad: Lois Farrakhan and the Nation of Islam*, Durham, NC: Duke University Press, 1996.

Gonzaga, Russell Reza-'khaliq; "One Nation Under Allah," *ColorLines* (Vol 5. No. 3), Oakland: ARC Publications, 2002.

Haddad, Yvonne Yazbeck and Lummis, Adair; *Islamic Values in the United States: A Comparative Study*, New York: Oxford University Press, 1987.

Haddad, Yvonne Yazbeck; *The Muslims of America*, New York: Oxford University Press, 1991.

Haley, Alex; *The Autobiography of Malcolm X*, New York: Grove Press, 1993.

Harrison, Christopher; *France and Islam in West Africa*, 1860-1960, England: Cambridge University Press, 1988.

Hasan, Asma Gull; *American Muslims: The New Generation*, New York: Continuum, 2000.

Lee, Martha; *The Nation of Islam: An American Millenarian Movement*, Syracuse, NY: Syracuse University Press, 1996.

Lewis, Bernard; "The African Diaspora and the Civilization of Islam", *The African Diaspora: Imperative Essays*, edited by Maritin L. Kilson and Robert I. Rotberg, Cambridge: Harvard University Press, 1976.

Lincoln, Eric; "The American Muslim Mission in the Context of American Social History," *The Muslim Community in North America*, ed. Earl H. Waugh et all, The University of Albert Press, 1983, p 224.

Macron, Marry Haddad; *Arab Americans and Their Communities of Cleveland*, Cleveland: Cleveland State University, 1978.

Maier, Mark H.; *The Data Game*, New York: M.E. Sharpe, 1995.

Martin, Tony; Race First: The Ideological and Organizational Struggles of Marcus Garvey and the Universal Negro Improvement Association, Westport: Green Wood Press, 1976.

Martinson, Paul Varo; *Islam : An Introduction for Christians*, translated by Stefanie Ormsby Cox, Minneapolis: Augsburg, 1994.

Masotti, Louis H. and Corsi, Jerome; *Shoot-out in Cleveland: Black Militants and the Police*, Washington: U.S Government Printing Office, 1969.

McCloud, Aminah Beverly; *African American Islam*, New York: Routledge, 1995.

Mirza, Harza; *Ahmadiyyah Movement: A History and Perspective*, New Delhi: Monahar Book Services, 1974.

Mohammed, Imam Warith Deen; *The Champion We Have In Common: The Dynamic African American Soul*, Illinois: W.D.M. Ministry Publication, 2001.

Muhammad, Elijah; *Message to the Black Man*, Chicago: Muhammad Temple No.2, 1965.

Nathari, Amina; *Islam In America*: 1995: 20 years A.E. (After Elijah), New Jersey: Sabree Publication, 1995.

Nurddidin, Yusuf; "African American Muslims and the Question of Identity," *Muslims on the Americanization Path?*, edited by Yvonne Yazbeck Haddad and Esposito, John L, New York: Oxford University Press, 2000.

Nyang, Sulyman; "Islam in the United States of America: A Review of the Sources," *Islam in North America: A Sourcebook*, edited by Michael A. Koszegi and J. Gordon Melton, New York: Garland Publishing 1992.

Plagenz, George; "Allah Be Praised From Union Ave," *The Cleveland Press*, October 19, 1974, p 5.

Quick, Abdullah Hakim; *Islam and the African in America: the Sunni Experience*, Ontario: Omni Print, 1997.

Qureshi, Regula B. and Qureshi, Saleem M; "Pakistani Canadians: The Making of a Muslim Community," *The Muslim Community in North America*, edited by Earl. H. Waugh et all, Alberta, Canada: The University of Alberta Press, 1983.

Raboteau, Albert J.; Slave Religion: *The "Invisible Institution" in the Antebellum South*, New York: Oxford University Press, 1978.

Reed, Ishmael; MultiAmerica: Essay on Cultural Wars and Cultural Peace, New York: Penguin Books, 1997.

Reed, Jr. Adolph; "The Rise of Louis Farrakhan," *The Best of the Nation*, edited by Victor Navasky & Katrina Vanden, New York: Nation Book, 2000.

Richburg, Keith; *Out of America*, New York: Basic Books, 1997.

Sanchez, Samantha and Galvan, Juan; "Latino Muslims: The Changing Face of Islam in America," *Islamic Horizons*, New York: Islamic Society of North America, July/ August 2002.

Scheer, Robert; Eldridge Cleaver: *Post-Prison and Writings and Speeches*, New York: Random House, 1968.

Selz, Michael, "Sam Quasem Tries to Ease Tensions Between Arab-American Grocers and the Blacks They Serve," *Plain Dealer*, January 3, 1999.

Sharif, Jafar; *Islam in India*, New Delhi: Oriental Books Reprint Corporation, 1972.

Suleiman, Michael; "Arab American: A Community Profile," *Islam in North America: a Source Book*, ed. Koszegi, Michael and Melton J. Gorden; New York: Grand Publishing, 1992.

Tabatab'i, Allamah Sayyid Muhammad Husayn; *Shite Islam*, translated by Seyyed Hossein Nasr; New York: State University of New York Press, 1975.

Tassel, David D. Van and Grabowski, John J; *Encyclopedia of Cleveland History*, Bloomington: Indiana University Press, 1987.

Tate, Sonsyrea; *Little X: Growing Up in the Nation of Islam*, New York: Harper Collins Publishers, 1997.

Ternikar, Farah; "Tribalism in Muslim America," *Islam in America: Images and Challenges*, ed. By Phylis Lan Lin; Indianapolis: University of Indianapolis, 1998.

The Islamic Affairs Department of the Embassy of Saudi Arabia, *Understanding Islam and the Muslims*, Washington, DC: The Embassy of Saudi Arabia.

Waldo, Dwight; *The Administrative State*, New York: Holms & Meier Publishers, 1984.

Wilkins, Roger; *Jefferson's Pillow: The Founding Fathers and the Dilemma of Black Patriotism*, Boston: Beacon Press, 2001.

Williams, Chancellor; *The Destruction of Black Civilization*. Chicago: Third World Press, 1987.

Wood, Peter H.; *Black Majority*, New York: W.W. Norton & Co., 1974.

Index

A

Abduh, Muhammad 134, 135
Abdul-Jabbar, Kareem 75, 87
Abdus-Shaheed, Muridiyah xii, 22, 67, 135
Abduwahab, Hajja N Akram 136
Abdurrahim, Al-Mansur 138
Abraham 6
Adenu Allahe Universal Arabic Association 61
Ahmad, Abbas xii, 84
Ahmad, Azzam 20
Ahmadiyyah 1-3, 23, 41, 42, 56-61, 63, 69-71, 99, 117, 145
Akeem, Ibrahim Abdul 45
Al-Amin, Jamil Abdullah 76, 85, 87, 132, 142
al-Farisi, Abdullahi 101, 105
Al khulafa ar-Rashiduna 13
Alcindor, Lewis 75
Ali (Prophet's son-in-law) 12, 13, 27, 43
Ali, Duse Muhammad 42
Ali, Muhammad 20, 42, 56, 74, 84, 123
Ali, Muhammed Younus 136
Ali, Timothy Drew 57
Ali, Yusuf 84, 88
Allah 5, 6, 7, 9, 10
Akram, Wali 3, 5, 40, 57, 59, 60-64, 66-68, 70, 71, 82, 93, 111, 136
American converts 14, 29, 35, 40, 46, 92
American Muslim Corporate Program 84
American Muslim Council 17, 46, 109
American Muslim Spokesmen 68
Amrah, Ahmad 103
Ansari, Ahmad Said xii, 96, 103
Ansari, Nazam 103
Ansari, Riaz 103
Arab world 89, 90, 96, 98
Asante Kere, Molefi 38, 39, 51, 141
Austin, Allan 35, 38, 50, 141

B

Bagby, Ihsan 29, 48, 127
Baldwin, James 38, 51
Bamba, Sheikh Ahmadou 92
Bangladesh 16, 95
Banna, Ahmad 108
Black Muslims 80, 81, 82, 98
Black Panther Party 75, 76, 80
Blyden, Edward W. 34, 50
Borchert, James xi
Brown, Claude 45, 53, 73, 75, 86, 87
Brown, H. Rap 45, 46, 75, 85, 87

C

Call & Post 63, 71, 73, 77, 82, 87, 88
Case Western Reserve University viii, 45, 100
Caucasian 14, 117, 122, 127, 128
China 16, 47, 89
Christ, Jesus 6
Christianity 5, 6, 12, 15. 31, 34, 41, 42, 50, 55, 119, 132, 142, 143
Civil Rights Movement 38, 41, 66, 73, 76
Civil War 31

Clarke, John Henrik 38, 51, 223
Clayde X 83
Cleaver, Eldridge 45, 46, 53, 76, 80, 87, 147
Cleveland Community Islamic School 23, 86, 94, 113
Cleveland News 1, 3
Cleveland State University vii, 80, 105, 111, 113, 145
Cory Methodist Church 45, 77, 79, 82
Cuyahoga Community College 100, 105

D

Damra, Fawaz 22, 108
Dannin, Robert 40, 51, 70, 71
Da'wa 9
Dervie, Salim 103
Diablo (the devil) 46, 85
Diouf, Sylviane 30, 36, 49, 50, 93, 142
Du Bois, W.E.B. 34, 35, 41, 42, 50, 143

E

El-Shabbaz, Malik 73
Essien-Udom, E. U. 38
Europe 16, 65, 90, 95, 117
Evans "Ahmad", Fred 80

F

Farrakhan, Louis 45, 53, 84, 85, 87, 123, 144, 146
Fellague, Ahmed 103
Fiqh 15, 91, 106

First Cleveland Mosque 1, 2, 3, 23, 60, 62, 84, 105, 136
Fisher, Allan 39, 51, 88
Five Pillars (Islamic teachings) 7-9
Fodio, Usman Dan 33

G

Garvey, Marcus 41, 42, 57, 70, 145
Greater Cleveland 2, 5, 6, 67, 94, 96, 99, 101-103, 108, 136

H

Halabi, Hana 136
Hamzah, Tariq 81-83, 85
Hamzah, Theodore 81, 82
Harlem 45, 61, 73, 75, 92
Hasan, Asma Gull 40, 51, 53
Hunwick, John 32, 50, 141

I

ibn Said, Omar 30
Ijma 10, 11
Indian Subcontinent 16, 94
Indonesia 14, 16, 100, 117, 120
Islamboli, Ramiz viii, 46, 101, 102, 135
Islamic Center of Cleveland 20, 26, 95, 96, 102-108, 111, 113, 117, 125, 136
Islamic Circle of N. America 1, 95
Islamic School of the Oasis 47, 85, 88, 93, 94
Islamic Society of N. America 48, 53, 93, 95, 101, 225
Israel 15, 96

J

Jihad vii, 9, 49, 69, 90, 109, 110, 142
Jones, LeRoi 75
Judaism 5, 6, 12, 15, 87, 119, 132

K

Ka'ba 8
King (Jr.), Martin Luther 48, 73, 76, 79

L

Lake Chad 16, 34
Laryea, Sheikh Masoud xii, 85, 94, 105, 110, 136
Lebanon 15, 99, 111, 135
Lewis, Bernard 38, 39, 51, 134,
Lomax, Louis 77, 80

M

Malaysia 14, 16, 90, 100, 117
Mali 31, 33, 34, 92
Malik, Daud Abdul 21, 46, 47, 85, 86, 93, 94
Malik, Sulayman Abdul 21, 23, 67, 71
Masjid Al-Haqq 21, 25, 85, 86, 93, 94, 138
Masjid al-Jami'h 18
Masjid Al-Islam 22, 26, 95, 105, 107, 113, 117
Masjid Al-Mu'min 22, 66, 67, 117, 125, 135
Masjid An-Nur 22, 25, 66, 67, 111, 113, 117, 128, 136, 138
Masjid Bilal 20, 83, 84, 94, 113, 116, 128, 138
Masjid Ummatullah 23, 25, 66, 113, 117, 128, 138
Masjid Warith Deen 23, 24, 25, 84, 88, 113, 116, 128, 138
Math-hab 15
Mecca 8, 19, 28, 30, 31, 35, 43, 64, 66, 94, 107, 136
Middle East 5, 14, 15, 17, 33, 39, 47, 89, 97, 99, 100, 104, 106, 108, 132, 133
Moer, Abdussamih 100, 105
Mohammedan (Muslim) 1
Morocco 14, 28
Moslem Ten Year Plan 5, 59, 61, 71, 81
Mosques vi, 1, 2, 17-20, 24-26, 28, 42, 46, 55, 56, 64, 66, 70, 76, 85, 90, 91, 94, 95, 98, 99, 101, 103, 105, 106, 111-113, 118, 124-128, 131, 137, 138
Muhammad, Amir N. Ali 37, 98, 223
Muhammad, Elijah 37, 45, 51, 74, 82-87, 123, 144
Muhammad, Fard 57
Muhammad (Prophet) 5, 10, 12, 26, 27, 43, 56, 58, 69, 109, 136
Muhammad, Walter Akim 45
Muhammad, Warith Deen 3, 20, 23, 24, 37, 50, 68, 83, 85, 123, 145
Murid 92, 93, 109
Muridiyah 93, 109
Musa, Mansa 31

Muslim Association of Cleveland East (MACE) 24, 26, 95, 108, 113, 117, 128
Muslim Student Association (MSA) 25, 99, 100-102, 111, 113
Muslim World 12, 15, 18, 28, 44, 46, 51, 52, 56, 69, 81, 91, 98, 132, 135

N

Nation of Islam 3, 25, 37, 38, 41, 45, 57, 62, 63, 73, 74, 76, 77, 81-88, 97, 106, 117, 123, 137, 143, 144, 147

Nawwash, Sheikh Salih xii, 105, 107, 112
Nigeria 33, 34, 44, 47, 50, 52, 85, 92, 93, 141
North Africa 14, 15, 17, 70, 91, 100, 103, 104, 132
North American Islamic Trust 101
Northwestern University 32

O

Omar, Ali viii, 85, 86, 88, 93, 94
Organization for Afro-American Unity 74

P

Pakistan 14, 16, 57, 64, 90, 95, 103
Palestinians 19, 96
Plain Dealer 1, 3, 5, 55, 71, 87, 88, 107, 110, 147

Q

Qiyas 11
Quick, Abdullah Hakim 36

R

Rahman, Anwar 108, 112
Rahman, Clyde 20, 83, 84
Ramadan 8, 10, 28, 30, 43, 81, 89, 108
Raza, Hasan 103
Reed, Ishmael 3

S

Sahabah 11
Samad, Khalid Abdul xii, 140
Saudi Arabia 8, 36, 64, 89, 91, 93, 109, 148
Senegal 14, 31, 33, 46, 47, 50, 92, 93, 109, 110
Shari'ah 6
Shi'a (*Shi'tes*) 12-14, 27
Siraj, Hussein 105, 127
South Africa 16, 92
Sufi 14, 15, 46, 58-60, 90, 92-94
Sulayman Nyang 44, 52, 87, 93, 97, 146

T

Temple No.18 81, 83, 84
The Plain Dealer 1, 3, 55, 71, 87, 88
Timbuktu 32, 50, 141
Toure, Askia Muhammad 75
Turkey 14, 15, 64-66, 89-91

U

Ummah 11, 12, 96
Uqbah Mosque 21, 46, 100-102, 113, 117, 125, 127, 128, 135
Uqbah Mosque Foundation 21, 46, 100-102, 113, 117, 125, 127, 135
United Islamic Society of America 61
United States xi, 2, 17, 19, 20, 35, 39, 45, 46, 48, 51, 57-59
U.S. Census Bureau 17

W

Williams, Chancellor 38, 51
World War-II 62, 65, 92, 94, 96

X

X, Malcom 38, 41, 42, 45, 46, 48, 49, 67, 73, 75, 77-81, 83, 86-88, 91, 109, 110, 123, 138, 142-144

Y

Ali, Yusuf 84, 88

Z

Zamzami, Qadi 104
Zakat 8, 91